'It is always good to find a book that does what it says in the title, and *Simply Brilliant* is one of these. Since the first edition, this book has been a permanent reference and is now a recommended read for all staff members.'

Noel Kelly FRSA, Chief Executive Officer/Director, Visual Artists
Ireland

'*Simply Brilliant* is packed with great advice and telling anecdotes. It's a must read for anyone who wants to simplify their life and get more done! And don't we all!'

Warick White, Managing Director of Coca Cola Australia/New
Zealand

'Fergus's ability to cut through the jargon and get to the heart of the matter is unparalleled. He has once again turned the complex into the simplex and in doing so making his hard won experience accessible to all. He is Simply Brilliant!'

Mike Nelles, Nelles & Associates Pty Ltd

'*Simply Brilliant* is a great book and proof that brilliant ideas don't have to be complicated. Fergus is an expert in getting things done and his rules to common sense are simple and effective!'

Raomal Perera, Entrepreneur and Visiting Professor, Entrepreneurial
Studies at Insead Business School

Simply Brilliant

Books that make you better

Books that make you better – that make you *be* better, *do* better, *feel* better. Whether you want to upgrade your personal skills or change your job, whether you want to improve your managerial style, become a more powerful communicator or be stimulated and inspired as you work.

Prentice Hall Business is leading the field with a new breed of skills, careers and development books. Books that are a cut above the mainstream – in topic, content and delivery – with an edge and verve that will make you better, with less effort.

Books that are as sharp and smart as you are.

Prentice Hall Business.
We work harder – so you don't have to.

For more details on products, and to contact us, visit
www.pearsoned.co.uk

Simply Brilliant

The competitive advantage of common sense

Third edition

Fergus O'Connell

PEARSON
Prentice Hall
BUSINESS

Harlow, England • London • New York • Boston • San Francisco • Toronto • Sydney • Singapore • Hong Kong
Tokyo • Seoul • Taipei • New Delhi • Cape Town • Madrid • Mexico City • Amsterdam • Munich • Paris • Milan

PEARSON EDUCATION LIMITED

Edinburgh Gate
Harlow CM20 2JE
Tel: +44 (0)1279 623623
Fax: +44 (0)1279 431059
Website: www.pearsoned.co.uk

First published in Great Britain in 2001
Second edition published 2004
Third edition published 2008

© Pearson Education 2001, 2004, 2008

The right of Fergus O'Connell to be identified as author of this work has been asserted by him in accordance with the Copyright, Designs and Patents Act 1988.

ISBN: 978-0-273-72077-5

British Library Cataloguing-in-Publication Data
A catalogue record for this book is available from the British Library

Library of Congress Cataloging-in-Publication Data
O'Connell, Fergus.
    Simply brilliant : the competitive advantage of common sense / Fergus O'Connell. — 3rd ed.
        p. cm.
    ISBN 978-0-273-72077-5 (pbk.)
        1. Executive ability—Problems, exercises, etc. 2. Common sense—Problems, exercises, etc.
    3. Simplicity—Problems, exercises, etc. 4. Management—Problems, exercises, etc. I. Title.
    HD38.2.O3 2008
    658.4'09—dc22
                                2008028876

10 9 8 7 6 5 4 3 2 1
12 11 10 09 08

Typeset in 10pt IowanOldStyle by 3
Printed and bound in Great Britain by Henry Ling Ltd, Dorchester, Dorset

The publishers' policy is to use paper manufactured from sustainable forests.

This book is dedicated to Sammy Goldstein

Contents

About the author   xi

Preface   xiii

Acknowledgements   xv

Introduction   xvii

01 Many things are simple   1

02 Know what you're trying to do   9

03 There is always a sequence of events   23

04 Things don't get done if people don't do them   55

05 Things rarely turn out as expected   99

06 Things either are or they aren't   109

07 Look at things from others' points of view   115

08 Get things done in the shortest possible time   149

09 Extreme time management   165

Afterword   179

Answers to questions and scores   185

Bibliography   191

About the author

Fergus O'Connell is one of the world's leading authorities on project management and getting things done in the shortest possible time. *The Sunday Business Post* has described him as having 'more strings to his bow than a Stradivarius'. He has a First in Mathematical Physics and has worked in information technology, software development and general management.

Fergus has spent much of the last 30 years doing, teaching, learning, writing or thinking about project management. In 1992 he founded ETP (www.etpint.com), which is now one of the world's leading programme and project management companies. His project management method – Structured Project Management / The Ten Steps – has influenced a generation of project managers. This method was used to plan and execute the Special Olympics World Games 2003, the world's biggest sporting event that year. His radical methods for shortening projects are in use by a growing band of devotees. His experience covers projects around the world; he has taught project management in Europe, North America, South America and the Far East. He holds two patents.

Fergus is the author of eight books (including this one), both fiction and non-fiction:

- *How To Run Successful High-Tech Project-Based Organizations* [1999]
- *How To Run Successful Projects In Web-Time* [2000]
- *How To Run Successful Projects: The Silver Bullet*, 3rd edition [2001]
- *Call The Swallow* [2002]

- *How To Do A Great Job: And Go Home On Time* [2005]
- *Fast Projects: Project Management When Time Is Short* [2007]
- *How To Get More Done: Seven Days to Achieving More* [2007]

The first of these, sometimes known simply as *The Silver Bullet* has become both a bestseller and a classic. *Simply Brilliant* – also a bestseller – was runner-up in the WH Smith Book Awards 2002. *Call The Swallow* was short-listed for the 2002 Kerry Ingredients Irish Fiction Prize and nominated for the Hughes & Hughes / Sunday Independent Novel of the Year. His books have been translated into 13 languages.

Fergus has written on project management for *The Sunday Business Post*, *Computer Weekly* and *The Wall Street Journal*. He has lectured on project management at University College Cork, Trinity College Dublin, Bentley College, Boston University, the Michael Smurfit Graduate School of Business and on television for the National Technological University.

He has two children and lives with his wife in France.

Preface

Much of my adult life has been spent rubbing shoulders with smart people. In college, in every job I've ever been in, in starting my own company, these smart people have been colleagues, bosses and peers. Because my background is in software development, many of these smart people have been at home in that discipline – a science that is immensely sophisticated, meticulous and complicated. I believe this experience is true not only of myself. More and more of us are finding our lives affected by these selfsame smart people and the things they make and do.

Over the years a suspicion has gradually been growing on me. It is a suspicion that I have been slow to voice. However, as the years have gone by, and as the evidence has accumulated, I have finally come to the conclusion that despite smartness, expertise, skill, experience, genius, in some cases some (many?) of these people are lacking in an essential skill.

That skill is what I refer to in this book as 'common sense'.

'The trouble with common sense,' the old saw goes, 'is that it's not all that common.' That has very much been my experience. Despite all the smarts that are floating around the place, a lot of dumb things get done. These are things which, if we only applied some of this pixie dust we call common sense, would never have been allowed to happen.

It is against this background that I have written this little book. It tries to set down a number of what one might grandly call 'principles' of common sense. Rather than trying to *define* common sense, it tries to identify a bunch of things which, if one were doing them, would be 'using common sense'.

I don't see these principles as being in any way absolute. Some other writer might have put forward a different set. However, I believe the principles given here can serve as a useful toolbox for attacking many of the problems that one encounters every day, be it in work or outside. Within work, I believe the application of these ideas will yield real benefits – hence the title.

To put things another way, this book may not be the only game in town, but it is *a possible* bag of pixie dust.

Acknowledgements

This book is a project that I have been nursing for a long number of years. I think there was a part of me that always thought it was too wacky for any publisher to be interested in. I would talk to people about it and – it may have been my imagination – they would smile uncomfortably, and begin to move warily away. That it has finally seen the light of day is the result of one woman's belief in and passion for the project. That woman is my editor at Pearson Education, Rachael Stock. When Rachael called me to say 'everyone loved it' – 'it' being the book proposal – I think what she was really saying was that everyone had been infected by her enthusiasm for it. Rachael has been the perfect editor and I thank her for giving me the chance to write my book. Samantha Jackson played the same role on this book. This is the third time we have worked together and each book has been a pleasure.

I would never have got to be a writer at all if it hadn't been for Viki Williams, and Viki played an unsung part in this book.

I learned a great lesson in common sense from my sister-in-law, Paula McHugh. John Brackett of Boston University taught me that things either are or they aren't. Dee Carri and Kevin Barrett in Elan Corporation are both major exponents of the art of common sense (people whom I call 'magicians', Kevin calls 'gladiators' and I have used his terminology in Chapter 4). My colleague, long-time friend and serious common-sense practitioner, Petra Costigan-Oorthuijs, created the 'strip board' example in Figure 4.7. Clare Forbes offered advice that was both wise and practical about the structure of the book and its chapters. If the book turns out to be usable, rather than ending up as 'shelfware', it will be in no small measure due to her suggestions. My colleagues at ETP – Mary Barry, Noel Kelly, Elaine Moore, Conor McCabe, Bernadette Coleman, Sean McEvoy and Harriet Cotter – all gave valuable input as to what should go into the book.

Finally, two people who taught me much of what I know about common sense are Hugh and Ferga. Thanks (again), guys.

Introduction

The book identifies what, I suppose, might grandly be called 'principles' of common sense. I'd rather think of it as giving a set of ideas – seven of them – which, if one applies one or more of the ideas, one is using common sense.

In keeping with the first of the seven ideas – that many things are simple – the book is simple. There are nine chapters. The first seven cover each of the seven ideas. The eighth chapter is about getting things done in the shortest possible time. The ninth chapter – a new one – is about using common sense in the crucial area of time management. Each chapter follows the same organization:

- For some chapters (2, 4 and 7) there are multiple-choice questions to get you thinking. In a sense, these questions test whether and how much you think in a common-sense sort of way.
- Then there is a spiel describing the particular idea.
- Next come some tools to help you apply the idea.
- Then there are examples of applying the particular idea. Sometimes the examples are simple applications of the particular idea. Sometimes the examples take several of the ideas and combine them together.
- Finally, there are some action points or things you could do to begin applying that particular idea in your daily life.

I'd like to know if you found the book useful or if it made any kind of difference. Or not! With that in mind you can e-mail me at fergus.oconnell@etpint.com with any brickbats or bouquets (or anything in between).

Finally, a note on terminology. I use the words 'project', 'venture' and 'undertaking' interchangeably in this book. They all are taken to mean something that you're trying to do.

01

Many things are simple

This chapter extols the virtues of simplicity in our thinking and encourages us to seek simple solutions.

The idea

I'll freely accept that some things in life are not simple. Putting a man on the moon, for example, or the Apollo 13 rescue were, I'm sure, immensely complex feats of engineering, mathematics, computing, rocketry and many other disciplines.

However, something you may have come across is the expression 'It's not rocket science'. Launching, flying and returning the Space Shuttle *is* rocket science and requires the application of a lot of complex scientific and technological thought. But most of us aren't flight directors at NASA and the things we do are definitely not rocket science. Too often, I believe we look for complex solutions when simple ones would be (a) much more appropriate, (b) much easier to find and (c) much simpler to implement.

Let's look at a couple of examples of complex solutions.

The European Union's Common Agricultural Policy

While I am European, I am not a great fan of the European Union (EU). I guess I've always leaned more towards the 'small is beautiful' end of things. Hence, I see the agglomeration of more and more European countries into a single great political/economic entity as not necessarily a good thing.

However, the EU is not without its benefits, perhaps the biggest one being that, for more than 50 years now, there hasn't been a war in Europe. While one has to get slightly lawyerish about this statement – 'not a *major* war in *Western* Europe' – it remains essentially true. And for this indeed we should be thankful, given that twice last century the continent witnessed the alternative.

"The things we do are definitely not rocket science."

That having been said, there are some things about the EU that are just plain appalling, and topping the list has to be the Common Agricultural Policy, or CAP for short.

Like many of these things, the CAP started off with a very laudable aim. It was conceived in the 1960s when the six original European Economic Community (EEC) countries were facing food shortages and imported much of their food. Some price supports and import levies were introduced in order to expand domestic production and reduce dependence on imports. In the following years, notwithstanding adequate supplies and higher self-sufficiency rates, this system was not dismantled and generated surpluses of many commodities.

Instead of reducing or removing price support, which was encouraging the production of those commodities regardless of market demand, the Council of Ministers, under pressure from producer lobbies, introduced new measures aimed at getting rid of production surpluses. Export subsidies, market withdrawals, wine distillation, destruction of perishable products were all introduced at a high cost to the EU budget and ultimately to consumers and taxpayers.

Like Topsy, the CAP 'just growed'. The problem it was meant to solve has long disappeared, but the policy has grown and expanded and mutated into the appalling mess that it is today.

The CAP is not a simple system. When I called the European Commission – God help me, in my innocence – 'to get a copy of it', I was told that it 'probably takes up about 15 filing cabinets'. And all for a system which a study by the European Commission – the organization which could be said to 'own' the CAP – slated on almost every ground imaginable – efficiency, inequity, the environment, food safety, food quality and food choice.

The design of computer systems

I think you'll agree that the design of most of the computer systems you come across is pretty crummy. (In fact, you could extend this discussion to a whole host of modern technological wonders – TV remote controls spring to mind – other than computer systems, but let's stay focused.) In his wonderful book *The Inmates are Running the Asylum*, Alan Cooper says: 'Most software vendors don't know how to make their programs easy to use (simple), but they sure know how to add features, so that is what they do.'

My own business is project management and the availability of software products such as Microsoft Project, which don't require a Cray 2 to run on, should have made my life easier. Has it? Anything but. The product is difficult and non-intuitive to use, with the result that I still end up relying on bits of paper. Microsoft could do the world a great favour by providing a slimmed-down, elementary (simple) set of features that just does the bare essentials. But no, as each new release comes from the Seattle factory, we see more and more complex features added.

Tools

If you are ever lucky enough to hear the Israeli scientist Eli Goldratt speak, he will almost certainly tell you what he calls 'one of the fundamental beliefs of science'. As he puts it, 'in reality there are no complex systems' or 'reality cannot be complex'. Therefore our first principle of common sense says that you need to shun complexity and seek simplicity. The following can all help you to do this.

- Look for simple solutions.
- Ask: 'What would be the simplest thing to do here?'

- See if you can describe something – an issue, a problem, a solution, a proposal – coherently in 25 words or less.

- Or can you do it in 30 seconds? This is sometimes called the 'elevator story' or 'elevator pitch', the idea being that you meet some important person in an elevator and you've got the flight time of the elevator to convey your message.

- Write down the issue/problem/solution/proposal.

- If you find you have ended up with a complex solution or idea, you have probably gone in the wrong direction. Go back and look again, this time in the simple direction.

- When you come up with something, ask: 'Is there a simpler way?'

- Get people to 'tell it like I'm a six-year-old'.

- Ask simple questions. Who? What? Why? Where? When? How?

- Ask for simple answers. This is particularly important when you are dealing with highly technical people.

- Remember the acronym 'KISS' – Keep It Simple, Stupid.

- Learn and use lateral thinking. The need for lateral thinking arises out of the way the mind works. The mind acts to create, recognize and use patterns. It does not act to *change* patterns. Lateral thinking is all about changing patterns. It is about escaping from old ideas and generating new ones. Lateral thinking involves two basic processes:
  - escape;
  - provocation.

Escape is about recognizing the current received wisdom with regard to something and then searching for alternative ways to look at or do that thing. Provocation is about finding those alternative ways.

"Lateral thinking is all about changing patterns."

■ Learn to think like Leonardo Da Vinci. In a book entitled *How to Think Like Leonardo Da Vinci*, the author, Michael Gelb, identifies what he calls 'the fundamentals of Leonardo's approach to learning and the cultivation of intelligence'. He crystallizes these in seven principles:

- **curiosità** being constantly curious about life and open to new learning;

- **dimostrazione** testing knowledge through experience, persistence and learning from mistakes;

- **sensazione** continually refining the senses (sight, hearing, smell, taste and touch) as a means of enhancing the experience of life;

- **sfumato** in Italian it means 'going up in smoke'. It refers to being able to be comfortable with paradox, uncertainty and ambiguity;

- **arte/scienze** developing 'whole-brain' thinking, i.e. the balance between art and science, logic and the imagination;

- **corporalita** it's the 'healthy body' part of 'a healthy mind in a healthy body' (*means sana in corpore sano*). It's about cultivating grace, fitness, poise and ambidexterity;

- **connessione** recognizing that everything is connected to everything else. (As Da Vinci put it: 'The earth is moved from its position by the weight of a tiny bird resting upon it.')

Examples

Example 1 Running a successful business

How do you run a successful business? They say it's complicated. There are business schools out there to enable you to do it properly. All manner of complex research has been done in the area. Could you describe it in five minutes, in a page, in a sentence?

You actually could, and Eileen Shapiro does precisely that in her book *The Seven Deadly Sins of Business*. She describes the professor entering her first finance class in business school and saying to the wannabe investment bankers and corporate executives: 'Don't run out of cash.' The recipe for a successful business? You bet it is.

Example 2 Marketing

Before I started my own company, I used to think that marketing was about sharp suits, power lunches, advertising hype and having to be nice to potential customers. I now realize it's one of the most complex, precise and demanding disciplines on earth. The key to being good at marketing is to be able to explain – *very simply* – why someone should buy what you sell.

If you can 'tell it to me like I'm a 6-year-old' then you will be a great marketeer.

Example 3 Lateral thinking

There's a story I heard which may well be apocryphal, but even if it is, it serves our purposes well at this point. It goes as follows.

A major US corporation built a new, high-rise corporate head-quarters. A few weeks after the building was fully occupied, the employees began to complain about the slowness of the elevators. Very quickly, the complaints reached epidemic proportions, so the company spoke to the architects of the building. Could the lifts be speeded up? Or increased in size? Sure, came the reply, but it would involve months of demolition, extension and reconstruction around the elevator shafts. It would be hugely disruptive to a large part of the workforce.

Supposedly, the story goes, the corporation did nothing to the elevator shafts. Instead, it placed full-length mirrors on every floor beside the elevator doors. The employees spent an extra few moments preening themselves and looking at one another in the mirrors, and the complaints faded away.

The point of the story? There must be a simple solution.

AND SO, WHAT SHOULD YOU DO?

1 Look for simple solutions.

2 Ask: 'What would be the simplest thing to do here?'

3 See if you can describe something – an issue, a problem, a solution, a proposal – coherently in 25 words or less.

4 Or can you do it in 30 seconds? This is sometimes called the 'elevator story' or 'elevator pitch', the idea being that you meet some important person in an elevator and you've got the flight time of the elevator to convey your message.

5 Write down the issue/problem/solution/proposal.

6 If you find you have ended up with a complex solution or idea, you have probably gone in the wrong direction. Go back and look again, this time in the simple direction.

7 When you come up with something, ask: 'Is there a simpler way?'

8 Get people to 'tell it like I'm a 6-year-old'.

9 Ask simple questions. Who? What? Why? Where? When? How? Which?

10 Ask for simple answers. This is particularly important when you are dealing with highly technical people.

11 Remember the acronym 'KISS' – Keep It Simple, Stupid.

12 Read Edward De Bono's book *Simplicity*.

13 Read any of Edward De Bono's books on lateral thinking.

14 Read *How To Think Like Leonardo Da Vinci*.

02

Know what you're trying to do

This chapter makes the age-old point that if you don't know what port you're sailing to, then any wind is a fair wind.

Questions

For answers to Questions, please see Answers to questions and scores on page 185.

Q.1 Somebody asks you to come to a meeting 'just in case we need your input'. What should you do?

(a) Refuse, on the basis that if they can't tell you the objective and your part in achieving that objective, it's pointless you being there.

(b) It depends who is asking you to come. A request from a senior is much different to a request from one of your peers. Go, if it's a higher-up, refuse (on the same grounds as in (a)) if it's a peer.

(c) Go regardless – it comes with the territory.

(d) Go regardless, but bring your in-tray with you so you can get some useful work done.

Q.2 Your company has landed a big project for a client. There is huge pressure to get the project completed on time. What's your first move?

(a) Send in the troops and tell them to start work.

(b) Agree with the client (in writing) completion criteria for the project, i.e. how we will *both* know (a) when this project is over and (b) that we have done a good job.

(c) Definitely don't do (b) on the basis that it will tie you down too much.

(d) Definitely don't do (b) on the basis that we don't have the time to waste on something we all know anyway.

Q.3 You've nearly completed an order for a customer when he phones you to ask for 'one little extra' but still with delivery as originally agreed. The 'one little extra' is actually reasonably significant. You are new to the company. The customer tells you that your predecessor always accommodated such requests. What do you do?

(a) Say 'yes'. Satisfying the customer is what it's all about.

(b) Ask the team to work some nights and weekends and have a moan with them about 'bloody customers'.

(c) Try to accommodate his desire for the end date not to change by adding more resources. If this fails, tell him the new end date.

(d) Use some of your contingency – assuming you have some – to satisfy the request.

The idea

'If you don't know what port you're sailing to,' the quote goes, conjuring up visions of sunny sea journeys in an unpolluted and empty Mediterranean, 'then any wind is a fair wind.'

The sentiment is so well known as to be clichéd. The quote is attributed to lots of different people. To the best of my knowledge it is not clear to whom attribution should go, other than the fact that it was uttered a long time ago.

To put it more mundanely, if you don't know what you're trying to do, it's going to be hard to do it.

Or let's have it from Lewis Carroll in *Alice's Adventures in Wonderland*. Alice asks the Cheshire Cat, 'Would you tell me, please, which way I ought to go from here?'

'That depends a good deal on where you want to get to,' said the Cat.

'I don't much care where,' said Alice.

'Then, it doesn't matter which way you go,' said the Cat.

Whether it's a meeting, a presentation, a day, a week, a year, a life, a house renovation, an ambition, or whatever, if you don't know what you're trying to achieve with that meeting, presentation, day, week, year, life, house renovation, ambition, or whatever, it's going to be hard to do it.

If you start a meeting and don't know what you're trying to get out of it, the chances of you actually getting something useful, never mind something you actually wanted, from it are pretty remote. At the other end of the scale, you've got one life. If, towards the end of it, you come to the conclusion that it wasn't the life you really wanted, it's too late.

It is before dawn as I write this page. When the sun comes up and the day begins, what am I hoping to achieve, what am I trying to do with this day? Don't know? OK, the day will be happy enough to just pass me by. Nothing wrong with that necessarily, except that if enough of them pass me by, that could be life passing me by.

Tools

In knowing what you are trying to do, there are really three issues you have to concern yourself with. These are:

- understanding what you're trying to do;
- knowing if what you're trying to do is what everyone wants;
- knowing if what you're trying to do has changed.

There is also one other tool I'd like to talk about and that is the notion of visualization.

Understand what you're trying to do

Somebody – your boss, say, or a customer – asks you to do something and you hare off straight away to do it. Right? Uh uh. Bad move.

What you really want to do, before you do anything else, is to understand *precisely* what they've asked you to do. The way to do this is to ask yourself these seven questions.

1 How will we know when we're finished?

2 What point in time constitutes its end point?

3 What physical things will it produce?

4 How will the quality of those things be determined?

5 What things are definitely part of this?

6 What things are definitely *not* part of this?

7 Are there any people issues that we need to be aware of in connection with this issue?

Doing this will give you a much clearer picture of what you've been asked to do. It will also often point the way forward in terms of what the next moves are.

Know if what you're trying to do is what everyone wants

Once you've figured out what it is you think you're trying to do, a good way to check on it is to do what is known as 'maximizing the win conditions of the stakeholders'. It's a fine phrase but what does it actually mean? Let's parse it from the end and see if we can find out.

'The stakeholders' are all those people who are going to be affected by what you're proposing to do. Each of those stakeholders has a set of one or more 'win conditions'. These are results that they would like to see emanate from the venture. Finally, putting it simply, 'maximizing the win conditions' means trying to find a result that gets the maximum amount of happiness for all of the stakeholders involved in the venture. You can think of 'understanding what you're trying to do' as finding *a possible* outcome to the undertaking, while this is about trying to find *the best* outcome.

We will see this notion again in Chapter 7.

Know if what you're trying to do has changed

Things change. What was important yesterday may not be important today. Or somebody has changed their mind about something. Or the industry or the business climate or the world has changed. Or somebody has forgotten something. Or didn't quite specify it correctly. You need to be watching for such changes to ensure that what you're doing – no matter how laudable it may have been in the past – hasn't suddenly been affected by one of these changes.

Perhaps the best way to do this is to go through the previous two procedures – 'Understand what you're trying to do' and 'Know if what you're trying to do is what everyone wants' – every day. This way, you increase your chances of catching changes, and you have an early warning system whose maximum width is 24 hours before you spot that something is not quite right.

Visualization

Visualization is all about trying to imagine what things will be like. Maybe, in some ways, daydreaming is a better word. Visualization is a powerful technique because it forces you to see what you're trying to do from many different perspectives. It can have dramatic and wide-ranging effects. In particular, visualizing what you're trying to do can have the following effects:

■ it helps you to identify the goal of a project or venture in the first place;

■ it tightens definition of that goal, identifying things which lie within the scope of the venture and things which lie outside it;

■ as we will see in the next example, it starts the planning process – the transition from the what (we are doing) to the how (we will do it);

■ it can be a huge motivator to all those involved in the project, as we paint the picture of where we are heading, what we will have achieved when we get there and what the journey there will be like.

"Visualization is all about trying to imagine what things will be like."

Here's a great example of visualization. It's taken from Martin Luther King's Washington speech in 1963.

I say to you today, my friends, so even though we face the difficulties of today and tomorrow, I still have a dream. It is a dream deeply rooted in the American meaning of its creed, 'We hold these truths to be self-evident, that all men are created equal'. I have a dream that one day on the red hills of Georgia, sons of former slaves and sons of former slave owners will be able to sit down together at the table of brotherhood. I have a dream that one day even the state of Mississippi, a state sweltering with the heat of injustice, sweltering with the heat of oppression, will be transformed into an oasis of freedom and justice. I have a dream that my four little children will one day live in a nation where they will not be judged by the color of their skin, but by the content of their character.

Examples

Example 1 Figuring out what you've been asked to do

Let's try to illustrate all of the above with an example. Let's assume your organization is expanding, you need more people and you've decided to run a job advertisement. Seems straightforward enough. Write the ad, run it and deal with the fallout from it. Let's see if applying our tools adds any value or provides us with any new insights.

Let's first attempt to understand what we're trying to do. How will we know when we're finished? This is actually a very interesting question, and the answer is not at all as obvious as it might first appear. Are we finished when the ad runs? Or when we've processed the results? Or run the interviews? Or hired the people? Or something else? In terms of the quality of what is delivered, if we spend large amounts of the company's money to run an ad, and we end up getting no responses, has this been a success? Do we care? (On the basis that it's not our money!) If our existing people see an ad, will there be issues about salary scales or job descriptions or conditions? If the hiring of the people lies within the scope of what we are doing, then we will have to involve other people – the Human Resources department, at the very least. I hope you can see that even by asking only a few of our questions, we find that this business of 'running an ad' is not at all as one-dimensional and well defined as it may have appeared at first glance.

Now let's assume we make some decisions. We assume that 'running the ad' will mean precisely that. It will encompass just the business of getting the ad into a particular newspaper. Anything else – processing the results, arranging and carrying out interviews, making job offers – will form part of a new little project. (Notice that this is completely arbitrary on our part – we could have chosen differently and still have been right.) So, we now know the answer to the question 'what point in time constitutes its end point?' It's when the ad appears in the *Hamster and Furry Rodent Weekly* or wherever it is you're planning to run it.

What physical things will it produce? Well, the ad itself, in some form that the newspaper can accept it in. (So somebody's going to have to find out. Notice how this thought process begins to bridge us from the *what* we are trying to do to the *how* we will do it.) The quality? Since we've decided that the level of response to the ad is outside the scope of what we're doing here, the quality is going to be measured purely by the fact that the ad represents our company well. Thus we can identify some measures, such as that it appears in a prominent part of the newspaper, that it sends out a good message about the company, that it contains no typos or misprints and so on. (So reviews and proofreading will be required. Notice again the bridge from the what to the how.)

And finally, in terms of people issues, we decide to make sure that anything that appears in the ad is in the public domain within the company. In other words, that nobody who already works in our company should be taken by surprise by the ad or find out things for the first time in it.

So, in summary, this venture involves running an ad which reflects well on the company and doesn't upset anyone already in the company, and we are finished when such an ad has run successfully in the chosen newspaper.

Now let's move on to establishing whether this is what everyone wants. Firstly, who is 'everyone'? Well, let's list them. There's:

- us;
- our boss – imagine her opening the paper and reading an ad that she, for whatever reason, turned out to be unhappy with. Our boss can perhaps act as a proxy for all other higher-ups – bigger bosses, shareholders, etc.;
- our existing employees;
- potential employees;
- our customers. Hey, we didn't start out expecting to see these guys here, but it's true. Existing and potential customers will read the ad, so it must say something to them.

And do these have win conditions? They sure do – see Figure 2.1 overleaf.

Figure 2.1 Stakeholders and their win conditions

Stakeholder	Win conditions
Us	■ Run ad that reflects well on the company and doesn't upset anybody. It also should communicate why the jobs on offer are so attractive that you'd have to be mad not to apply
Our boss	■ The ad sends out a positive message about the company
Existing employees	■ Doesn't upset anybody – uses only material that is in the public domain ■ Sends out a message that the company is one that people want to work for
Potential employees	■ Sends out a message that the company is one that people want to work for
Our customers	■ Sends out a message that the company is expanding and is a good company to do business with

I think you'll agree that this gives us a lot more insight into the nature of the ad we will write.

Finally, over the duration that this little project runs, nothing might change. Or it could equally happen that we decide to run it in other newspapers, or include other jobs in the ad as well as those in our department, or any number of other changes. We need to be alert to these over the life of the project.

Example 2 Meetings

Here's another example of knowing what you're trying to do.

Survey after survey affirms that most managers consider meetings to be the single biggest waste of their time. I have a friend who writes the minutes of meetings *before* the meeting. She has done this for years. In doing this she is focusing very clearly on the result she is trying to get from the meeting. She is saying, 'Here's how I will know when this meeting has achieved its objectives.'

This idea of 'what result are we trying to achieve?' is one that can be extended to all sorts of things:

▨ presentations;

▨ customer visits or sales calls;

▨ project status reports – write it *before* the period to which it is going to refer. Will having it in front of you keep you focused? You bet it will;

▨ the day ahead of you.

Example 3 Setting goals

The visualization tool is probably the best way I know to go about setting goals, be they business or personal ones. And this notion is not a new idea. Nearly 500 years ago, Pope Leo X complained about Leonardo Da Vinci: 'Here is a man, alas, who will never do anything, since he is thinking of the completion of his painting before he has started.' This idea of thinking about the end is also enshrined in one of Stephen Covey's '7 habits'. Habit 2 is 'Begin with the end in mind'. Visualization is a great way of doing precisely that.

"In daydreams we run little movie clips in our heads."

In a sense we are all familiar with visualization. If we've ever daydreamed, then we've been engaging in visualization. In daydreams we run little movie clips in our heads and in them we see ourselves doing things we really want to do. To begin setting personal goals, the best way to start is to picture what life will be like when that particular goal is achieved. Here are the kind of questions you could ask yourself to get the daydream (or movie clip) rolling.

- There will come a day when this goal has been achieved. What will life be like on that day?

- How will you feel?

- What will your ambitions/hopes/dreams be on that day?

- Will your standard of living have changed? If it is a business goal, will your position within the organization have changed?

- Will you have power, capabilities or other assets that you don't have at the moment?

- How will you spend your days?

- What will a typical day be like? What will be your routine? Your schedule? Think through such a day from getting up in the morning to when you go to bed at night. Who will you meet? Where will you eat your meals? What will you do, i.e. how will you occupy your time? Will this make you happy?

- Are there other people who will be affected by this goal? Who are they? (From a business point of view, think bosses, peers, customers, subordinates, team members, other parts of the organization. From a personal point of view, there are nearest and dearest, family, friends, acquaintances.)

- How will these other people be affected by the goal? What will reaching this goal mean to each of them?

- Why do you want to achieve this goal?

- Do the other people who will be affected by the goal have motivations with regard to the goal? Are these positive, neutral or negative motivations?

- What will other people be saying about you? Both the people who are affected by the goal and those who aren't affected but who know you.

- What recognition, if any, are you hoping to achieve in going for this goal?

- Will your view of yourself have changed? If so, how?

- Will you have changed as a person? If so, how?
- Do you think it is a difficult task you have set yourself?
- Could it fail?
- How would you feel then? What would you do?
- What would you like to do after you have achieved this goal?
- What would be the best possible outcome to this venture?

Example 4 Looking for simple causes

This example combines what we have learned in principles 1, many things are simple, and 2, know what you're trying to do.

One of the things we do in our company is project rescues. A few years ago I was asked to do one on a large, complex project that was adrift from both a budgetary and an elapsed time point of view. When I say the project was large, there were bits of it being done in a dozen countries. When I say it was complex, its purpose was to develop a very sophisticated software product.

On the first day I arrived on the scene, the project manager handed me six large folders, each about three inches thick, and each bulging with paper. 'You'll need to read these by way of background,' he said. Trying to conceal my dismay, I asked instead if he could tell me the story of the project. Principle 2 tells us that one possible reason the undertaking could have got into trouble is because the project goal hadn't been clearly defined. Maybe this was the case here. If not, maybe I would have to begin reading the half-yard of paper.

As it turned out, the project goal *hadn't* been properly defined. Six months into the project, the requirements and high level design were to have been completed and agreed so that software development could start. Not only were they not agreed, they were only partially written. Without going any further, we had unearthed the main reason why the project had gone AWOL.

As a footnote to this story, I once bid for another piece of project rescue business. I reckoned that in bidding five days of my time plus expenses, I would get the job done, come up with all the answers, get the report written, have a bit of contingency and make some profit. I didn't get the job. Subsequently I learned it had gone to one of the big consulting companies which had put a consultant in for two months. The theory seemed to be that complex projects required complex reasons for them to go wrong. This has *never* been my experience.

AND SO, WHAT SHOULD YOU DO?

1 Keep a list of the things you're trying to do – your 'projects'.

2 Use the tools we have described in the 'Tools' section of this chapter to analyse new things as they come along, and before adding them to your list of projects.

3 Check your list of projects regularly – ideally every day, worst case, every week – to see whether changes have occurred to your projects' goals. If there have been changes, you need to re-run the 'maximize the win conditions of the stakeholders' analysis.

03

There is always a sequence of events

This chapter shows that in order to do anything, there needs to be a sequence of events. Knowing this gives you the skills to plan, prioritize, accelerate projects and get many things done at the same time. It also shows why 'firefighting' can become the exception rather than the rule.

The idea

A few years ago, two people I know decided to take their children to Disneyland Paris. They explained their plan to me. It went like this. They would fly to Paris on Friday evening, arriving late. On Saturday morning, after breakfast, they would travel out from central Paris to Disneyland, spend the day there, visit all the good rides, come back, put the children to bed with a babysitter, have a bath to wind down, dress up, go out and have a nice relaxing dinner.

My immediate reaction was, 'That's gonna be one long day.' I guess it's the project manager in me, but it sounded to me like that Saturday wouldn't come to a close until well into Sunday. When I mentally strung all the tasks together, there seemed to be an awful lot going on there. When I did it on paper, my suspicions were confirmed. Here's what their Saturday was going to look like. Best case.

Depart hotel	9:00	With kids in tow, you'll be doing well if you achieve this.
Paris – Disneyland	9:00 – 11:00	
A day at Disneyland	11:00 – 19:00	Has to be a minimum of eight hours.
Disneyland – Paris	19:00 – 21:00	
Kids to bed	21:00 – 23:00	You can't just rush them off to bed when you get back.
Bath to wind down	23:00 – 24:00	Has to be at least an hour to get the value of it at all.
Dress up	24:00 – 01:00	It's now Sunday.
Find/get to restaurant	01:00 – 01:30	Assuming there's one that's open in the middle of the night! Hey, it's Paris – there's bound to be!

Nice relaxing dinner	01:30 – 04:30	Say 3 hours. At this stage the diners will have been up for close on 24 hours! Relaxed? I'd say they'll be comatose!

The point of this story is not to show that anyone was stupid. The point is that there is always a sequence of events, and many people either don't realize this or, if they do, don't seem to understand the implications of the sequence of events.

For some reason – I think it's something I got from my father – I'm very precise and, I guess, old-fashioned about time. If I tell somebody I'll meet them at 3 o'clock, I'll be there before 3.00. If they're not there at 3.00, I'll quickly begin to assume there's a problem. It's taken me a long time to realize that very few people are like me in this respect. And the difference, I've come to believe, is that very few people think in terms of a sequence of events.

Somebody agrees to meet you at a specific time. In general, in my experience, they don't take into account other meetings, things running over, getting across town, finding an unfamiliar place, getting a parking place, all things which can blow their appointment with you completely out of the water. I once worked at a company where people would wander into a meeting, say on a Wednesday, and ask, 'Is this the Monday marketing meeting?' This was my sequence-of-events theory gone mad.

"Quite simply, without sequences of events, nothing gets done."

The overwhelming reason why sequences of events are so important is because, quite simply, without sequences of events, nothing gets done. Let's say you're buying a house and the estate agent phones you and says, 'The owners of the house like your offer – it looks like we have a deal on our hands.' 'Great,' you say. 'Yeah, it is great,' he says and the call finishes. Now, if that is all that happens, nothing will get done. Because maybe the estate agent is waiting for you to make the next move, and you think his is the next move, and so a Mexican standoff ensues. If, however, you ask, 'So what happens next?' or he volunteers, 'So, here's what has to happen now,' then this is the cue for you and him to build a sequence of events.

Maybe you would never let this happen if you were buying a house, or engaged in some other important personal event, but how many times have you gone to a meeting where the following has happened? There is a complete meeting of minds. Everybody is agreed that the issue needs to be resolved and the way forward is decided. Then we all file out of the room. And hey, surprise surprise, nothing gets done. Nothing gets done because no sequence of events gets built. Or worse still, because nobody summarizes (ideally in writing) the actions arising from the meeting, everybody builds their own version of the sequence of events.

In her book *The Seven Deadly Sins of Business,* Eileen Shapiro discusses the reasons that companies get into trouble. The first 'deadly sin' is that too many companies identify an aggressive goal or vision or targets, then pay scant attention to 'how' those targets/that goal/those visions will be achieved. She is saying precisely what we are saying. If there is no sequence of events, nothing gets done.

A different way of thinking about all of this is to say that sequences of events are our best shot at understanding what will happen in the future. Which is just a complicated way of saying that sequences of events are *plans,* or, to be slightly more precise, sequences of events are the foundations of plans. And good sequences of events are the foundations of good plans.

How was some great undertaking, say D-Day, planned? Primarily because many many people built large, complicated, interconnected sequences of events.

If we know what we are trying to do (from Chapter 2) and can build sequences of events to do it, we are well on the way to getting lots of the things we want to do, done. The next question then is, what tools are there that can help us to build sequences of events? It turns out that there are seven of them:

1 Make the journey in your head.

2 Do it in as much detail as possible.

3 Use knowledge and assumptions.

4 Count the bricks in the wall.

5 There always has to be another way.

6 Record what actually happens.

7 Look for connections.

We discuss them in turn in the next section.

Tools

Make the journey in your head

When people were planning D-Day, nobody said (or if they did, we'd like to think that they were hastily overruled), 'Let's just send five divisions over there and see how they get on.' Instead the planners tried to think through how they would get from their current situation to the goal they had identified. They imagined/visualized/speculated/wrote down the sequence of events that would take them forward. The cause and effect. How each event or job would lead on to the next one until eventually, strung in a long chain, the events (or jobs) led from the start point to the destination. (I will often use the word 'job' here as it is (a) a well-understood word and (b) has a healthy sense of work ethic about it!)

Do it in as much detail as possible

The next important thing to bear in mind is the level of detail in which the sequence of events is described. The D-Day people didn't just say:

1 Start.

2 Rustle up five divisions.

3 Ship them to Normandy.

4 Get them ashore.

5 The end.

While at its highest level of abstraction the plan may have indeed looked like this, for it to have been in any way valid or usable it needed to be worked down to *as much detail as could possibly be imagined.* 'The devil is in the detail,' the old saw goes, and how true it is. It is only when we burrow down into the detail, it is only as we imagine ('make the journey in our heads') the various events taking place, and how the result of one event is then the start point for the next event, that we can unearth all the potential obstacles that lie up ahead. For my money, in most of the situations we encounter these days, a level of detail (or breakdown) where every job can be measured in the range of 1–5 person-days is what you need to be aiming for.

Use knowledge and assumptions

Of course, you may object and say, 'But I can't know all the events, I can't know all the detail.' And this is indeed true. So then the rule is simple. Where you have knowledge, use it. Where you don't, where – in the course of your mental journey – you come up against something and you have no idea what comes next, make some assumption. For example, how did the Allies know what kind of opposition they would face on Omaha Beach? Answer is, they didn't – for sure. But they had some knowledge, based on intelligence, reconnaissance and so on. For the rest they made assumptions. And these assumptions enabled them to continue to chain together sequences of events.

Count the bricks in the wall

Don't forget that things may have to be done more than once. You may be involved, for example, in something that has to take place at several of your company's sites. In that case, once you've identified the sequence of events once, you can essentially duplicate it for the other situations. This tool is about knowing how much 'stuff' has to be done.

There always has to be another way

'There's more than one way to skin a cat,' the saying goes. This tool says that there is always more than one possible sequence of events. Once you've figured out what you're trying to do (principle 2, know what you're trying to do), there are endless ways of getting there. In keeping with principle 1, many things are simple, we will always be looking for the simpler ways to do things, but this tool is also about determination and about never giving up looking for ways to do things.

Brainstorming is a powerful way of doing this. At the risk of telling you things you already know, do it in two passes. First of all, try to come up with as many ways as you can to solve the particular problem. Every idea is allowed at this stage. No idea, whether possible or impossible, wacky or sensible, vastly expensive or free, realistic or unrealistic, civilized or uncivilized, is ruled out. Write them all down, say on a flip-chart page. Then go back over the list and select those which meet certain criteria that you have set.

Record what actually happens

All the previous tools assumed you were starting from a blank sheet of paper. Often this is the case; the particular thing you are doing has not been done before and you are setting off into the great unknown. More often though, I think, we are doing things that *have* been done before. (D-Day, for example, learned many lessons from the disastrous amphibious raid on Dieppe two years earlier.) Then it should be possible to draw on other people's experience to build the sequence of events; our team may know things, or our peers, or somebody somewhere in the organization.

Even if that is not the case, that shouldn't stop you from quickly building up your own bank of knowledge as your venture unfolds. The table below shows a form for doing precisely that.

Phase	Planned		Actual		Difference	
	Elapsed % (days)	Work % (person-days)	Elapsed % (days)	Work % (person-days)	Elapsed % (days)	Work % (person-days)
Total						

In the leftmost column, you write down the major events, phases or jobs that took place in your undertaking. They might be things like 'requirements gathering', 'design', 'planning' and so on. Then there are three sets of four columns. The three sets are for (a) what you planned, (b) what actually happened and (c) the difference between the two. The blocks of four columns enable you to enter:

■ the elapsed time for that particular phase (planned, actual and the difference between the two);

- the elapsed time as a percentage of the overall elapsed time (you calculate this when the project is over and you know what the final elapsed time was). Again you do planned, actual and difference;

- the amount of work that went into each phase (planned, actual and difference);

- the work in each phase as a percentage of the overall amount of work in the project (again, you calculate this when the project is over and the final amount of work is known; there are planned, actual and difference as before).

An example of a completed form is shown in Figure 3.2 overleaf.

The material captured in this way is like treasure in heaven. (This statement is true even if you are at the beginning of your data-gathering career and have only one completed project in your databank.) The next time you come to plan something that is even remotely similar, you will find that you are able to get useful information from your databank. In addition, if you are asked to review other people's plans, you can compare what they are proposing with what is in your databank, and almost always draw useful conclusions.

Look for connections

Leonardo Da Vinci is only one of the world's thinkers who has made the observation that everything is connected to everything else. The theme recurs again and again in his writing. Here is just one example: 'Every part is disposed to unite with the whole, that it may thereby escape from its own incompleteness.' In generating sequences of events, one of the most useful things you can do is to look for connections between the sequences. Such connections may enable you to move several things along at once or accelerate one sequence by carrying out an activity in another.

Figure 3.2 A completed project knowledge form

Phase	Planned				Actual				Difference			
	Elapsed (days)	% (2)	Work (person-days)	% (3)	Elapsed (days)	% (5)	Work (person-days)	% (6)	Elapsed (days)	%	Work (person-days)	%
Requirements	40	26	27	4	15	14	34	6	-25	-63	7	26
Design (prototype)	14	9	22	4	15	14	33	6	1	7	11	50
Coding	32	21	184	30	53	48	164	30	21	66	-20	-11
System test (4)	60	39	115	19	47	43	159	29	-13	-22	44	38
Technical writing	84	55	99	16	88	80	88	16	4	5	-11	-11
Contingency	14	9	103	17	0	0	0	0	-14	-100	-103	-100
Project management	140	91	46	8	110	100	55	10	-30	-21	9	20
Total	(1)	(1)	596	98	(1)	(1)	533	96			-63	

(1) Adding these doesn't necessarily make sense since some of the phases of the project overlapped
(2) As a percentage of the total elapsed time, i.e. 154 days
(3) As a percentage of the total work, i.e. 610 person-days
(4) Estimated elapsed includes both writing the tests and carrying them out. Effort includes this plus bug fixing
(5) As a percentage of the total elapsed time, i.e. 110 days
(6) As a percentage of the total actual work, i.e. 554 person-days

These, then, are the seven tools that enable us to build a sequence of events. It has to be said that many people never go to the trouble of building sequences of events. They feel it is too much effort. (It isn't.) Or they feel that they can't. (They can.) Or that the effort far outweighs the benefit. (Not true either). For these people, the term 'firefighting' has been coined.

"Sometimes unexpected things do happen and there are real firefights."

Firefighting is the situation where some unexpected thing happens and effort – sometimes enormous effort – has to be put in to sorting it out. Don't get me wrong. Sometimes unexpected things do happen and there are real firefights. But many fire-fights need never have occurred if only people had exercised the grey matter and gone to the trouble of building a sequence of events.

Finally, just as a footnote, if your business is project manage-ment, you'll probably have deduced by now that a sequence of events is remarkably similar to what you would call a work breakdown structure or WBS.

Examples

Example 1 Estimating

It may be that one of the things you have to do in your job is that exciting blood sport known as estimating. I call it a blood sport because in estimating you have to predict the future. Then, based on how well or how badly you did this, your career progression and success will, to a greater or lesser extent, be determined. In the past I have taught estimating, and one of the things I often did during those classes was to hold up a schedule (which was based on estimates) in one hand and a lottery ticket in the other and ask the class, 'What do these have in common?' (Somebody once muttered, 'If I won the lottery I wouldn't have to do any more of these stupid schedules!') What they have in common is that they are both predictions of the future. We'd all like to feel that when we produce an estimate the odds on it happening are better than those of a lottery ticket, but I've definitely seen estimates where the smart money would have to have been on the lottery ticket!

The tools we have described above are the things you need to help you build accurate, resilient estimates. In general, when estimating, people are concerned with three things:

■ How long will something take? (What is its duration or elapsed time?)

■ How much work is involved in something? (Work is sometimes referred to as 'effort'.)

■ How much will something cost? (What is its budget?)

Notice too the very important fact that duration and work are not the same. Duration is how long something will take; work is how much effort is involved in that particular thing. For instance, an hour-long meeting involving six people has a duration of one hour, but an effort (work) of six person-hours. In my experience, confusion between these two quantities is the source of much human unhappiness. Imagine, for example, your boss comes in, flips a report on to your desk, and asks you, 'How long would it take you to have a look at that?' You look at it, think for a moment, and reply, 'Oh, about an hour.' Now if you've given effort but your boss thought he got duration, can you see the potential for unhappiness? Your boss thinks he's going to get your comments back within the hour. You know, looking at the backlog you have (300 unread e-mails – that sort of thing!), that it will be weeks before you get to his benighted document.

I've seen all sorts of scientific and pseudo-scientific ways of doing estimating in different disciplines. Barry Boehm's *Software Engineering Economics* contains a comprehensive treatment of it if you're a software person. However, for my money, nothing compares with the following description of estimating – a description that ends up defining both the process of estimating and the finished product. It's taken from Eberts and Ilott's *My Indecision is Final* and describes the preparations Sir Richard Attenborough had to make prior to shooting his movie *Gandhi*.

> *He [Attenborough] had to shoot the film during the cool season in India, starting in November and finishing the following April or May. (The summer would simply be too hot: a film crew could not function in 110 degree heat.) But to start in November he had to make preparations now, six months ahead: hiring the cast and crew, building the sets, sorting out the costumes, getting all the permissions needed to shoot in India, shipping the equipment and so on. The tasks, known as pre-production, are fairly straightforward if you are shooting in your own country, but are horrendously complicated when you are shooting overseas. To take a simple example, if you are going to fly in 125 people to make a movie, you have to book the hotel rooms and pay for them, or at least put down some sort of deposit, well in advance. **That means knowing now exactly where you will want each of those 125 people to be on any given day over the four or six months that the film will be shooting**.* [Emphasis added.]

So, if you are charged with estimating, this is what you must do. Establish, using the tools we described earlier in this chapter, what everyone is doing every day of the venture. (In Chapter 4, we will describe a tool known as a strip board which is used in the movie-making industry to do precisely this.) Then it becomes a straightforward matter to estimate:

- how long;
- how much work;
- how much money.

Figure 3.3 Estimating work and using assumptions

ID	Task name	Work	Predecessor	Notes
		44 days		
1	**1 The Project**			
2	1.1 START	0 days		
3	1.2 Project planning and scoping meeting	9 days	2	9 people for 1 day
4	1.3 Produce requirements document	27 days	3	
5	1.3.1 Research user requirements	7 days		
6	1.3.1.1 Gather info on competitive products	0.5 days		Charlie'll do it
7	1.3.1.2 Review with marketing	2 days	6	Assume 3 marketing people and Charlie @ 1/2 day each gives 2 days' work
8	1.3.1.3 Identify users	0.5 days	7	Marketing guy – his estimate
9	1.3.1.4 Prepare user questionnaires	2 days	8	Charlie says he'll do it. Take him a coupla days
10	1.3.1.5 Distribute questionnaires	0.5 days	9	An admin person. Estimate is on the basis that 1/2 day is the smallest unit we recognize
11	1.3.1.6 Retrieve questionnaires	0.5 days	10FS+1 wk	Half-a-day's work chasing. Probably 5 days elapsed time to get it done
12	1.3.1.7 Analyse information	1 day	11	Charlie and a marketing person @ 1/2 day each
13	1.3.2 Write requirements document	9 days	12	Charlie. Use company standard 9 section format @ 1 day per section

ID	Task	Duration	Pred	Notes
14	1.3.3 Review cycle	10.5 days	13	
15	1.3.3.1 Circulate	0.5 days		Admin person – basis for estimate is same as for 'Distribute questionnaires' above
16	1.3.3.2 Individual review	2.5 days	15	5 reviewers, 1/2 each, allow 1 week elapsed time in which it has to happen
17	1 3.3.3 Review meeting	3 days	16	Charlie and 5 reviewers @ 1/2 day each
18	1.3.3.4 Changes to document	2.5 days	17	Charlie – his estimate
19	1.3.3.5 Circulate again	0.5 days	18	Same as earlier 'Circulate'
20	1.3.3.6 Second review	1.5 days	19	5 reviewers, 1–2 hours each, try to do it ASAP – so give reviewers a deadline to respond with comments
21	1.3.4 Sign-off	0.5 days	14	Assume there will be no substantial changes. Admin person chases sign-offs
22	1.3.5 Requirements complete	0 days	21	
23	1.4 Produce system/acceptance test plan	8 days	4	
24	1.4.1 Research	5 days		
25	1.4.2 Write navigation tests	3 days	24	
26	1.4.2.1 Define test sequence	1 day		
27	1.4.2.2 Write test scripts	1 day	26	
28	1.4.2.3 Define expected results	1 day	27	
29	1.4.3 Write functionality tests	0 days	25	

Figure 3.3 on the previous page shows an example of estimating work and using assumptions (contained in the field headed 'Notes').

From the information in Figure 3.3 it would be possible to work out elapsed times – provided we knew people's availability. In addition, if we knew labour rates it would be possible to work out what things are costing. In the next chapter (Figure 4.7), we will see estimates laid out in a different way, on a strip board. Notice too that there's another example of estimating at the beginning of this chapter. We did it when we planned the Disneyland Paris trip. It's all there – jobs, elapsed times, assumptions, who's doing what, the works.

Example 2 Meetings

Let's say, for example, you're going to a meeting. Are you just at the mercy of whatever pops up at the meeting or can you do a bit better than that? The question is rhetorical because of course you can do better than that. For starters, you can decide what result you want to get from the meeting (principle 2) and then you can figure out how you might get it (principle 3).

Let's say the meeting is with a client and it's a difficult topic – it's about rebuilding a relationship that's gone off the rails. Not that anything particularly disastrous happens, just that it is perhaps at times mishandled, incorrect perceptions are allowed to spring up and fester and, generally, the thing isn't given professional tender loving care.

So you start by asking, 'What are we trying to get from the meeting?' An order? Hardly. Even if by some bizarre turn of fate they offered you one, you should almost (I said 'almost'!) be thinking in terms of declining it. Your emphasis today is on rebuilding the relationship. And on the basis that Rome wasn't built in a day, maybe you decide that the best you can hope to get today is to give them a feeling that you care. You want them to know, at the conclusion of the meeting, that you want to do business with them in the future and that you have value which you think you can add to their business. But you don't want it to be a sales pitch.

Let's say there are two of you going – you, because you have inherited the account, and your boss. You have asked for the meeting. The guys are giving you 20 minutes. (The detail is somewhat unimportant here except to illustrate things. What's important is how you have clearly set out what you do and don't hope to get from the meeting.) Now the sequence of events. You discuss it with your boss beforehand and settle on something like the following.

1 Your boss will open the meeting. He will thank them for taking the time out, explain that the purpose is to begin the process of rebuilding something which has been neglected. He will explain how you think you can still add value and how you hope to be a valuable supplier to them in the future. Then he will give them an opening to have a gripe.

2 You assume they will take the opportunity and that this will be the greater part of the meeting.

3 You agree that you will take their gripes on the chin, not trying to give excuses or correct them even if they're wrong. You may occasionally tell them of steps you have taken and things you have put in place to fix some of the problems they describe. Your boss will lead and you'll take notes.

4 You decide you'll allow the first three items to take at most 15 minutes so that you have a few minutes to close and get out within the 20 minutes they gave you.

5 Since every meeting should end with some kind of action – to keep the chain of events unbroken – you might mention to them that you plan to bid for the next piece of business that comes out (action on you) or tell them not to forget you next time they're looking for a blah supplier (action on them).

6 Finally, you'll thank them for their input, remind them of the value you can add, reiterate that you want to put the past behind you and move forward into what will be, it is hoped, a better relationship for both parties. Then you will say your goodbyes.

In terms of your goal, this should get you there. If it all goes horribly wrong, there's probably not much you can do except to get out with as much of your dignity intact as possible.

Again, the details are less important than the idea of using the two principles – figure out what you're trying to do and then put a sequence of events in place to do it.

Example 3 Dealing with lots of things / prioritizing

You may be trying to do a bunch of things. If you haven't established a sequence of events for each one, it's quite likely you'll end up flitting from one to the other, never sure (a) if you're progressing things and (b) if you're progressing the right things.

Once you have a sequence of events for each of the things you're trying to do, all of this changes. Then each sequence of events is like a stack of jobs to be done. By taking the top item from each stack you progress that particular thing forward. If you take the top item from every stack, everything gets moved forward. Even more usefully, when new things come winging in from outfield, you can check them against those stacks you're working with and see if they are relevant to things going on in the stacks. If they are, you can deal with them. If not, you can put them to one side. (Thus the best way to deal with an inbox is as follows: screen it for anything that needs dealing with straight away, i.e. that is relevant to one of the stacks you have going, otherwise leave it in a pile to be cleared once a week, once a fortnight, once a month – the longer the interval the better, in my view.)

If, in addition to all of this, you are good at prioritizing, you can restrict the number of things you concentrate on (and hence the number of stacks you have on the go) to the bare minimum that will make the biggest difference. (One suspects an 80/20 rule is operating here – do 20 per cent of the things and get 80 per cent of your job done.) To be good at prioritizing, just do the following: look at all the things you have on the go and ask yourself the question, 'If I could only do one thing, what would it be?' Having answered it, take the remaining items and ask the question again. Do this until all items have been assigned a priority. Try to ensure that two items don't have the same priority, because then it's not really a priority, is it?

Finally, as we pointed out in the 'Tools' section above, having sequences of events for each of the things you're trying to do means that you can look for connections between things. Something that you plan to do for thing A may also have an effect on thing B. Then you will be very keen to do it and it should shoot right to the top of your priority list. Conversely, if taking something from stack A will have a negative effect on something else, you may want to analyse it a bit more carefully before proceeding.

Example 4 Speeding things up

Having a sequence of events for each of the things you are trying to do also means that you can accelerate them. You know how it goes. There's something we're trying to do. It invariably involves other people. We do our bit, we give it to them and there it often hangs in some form of suspended animation.

But if we have a stack of events, we can look further down the stack rather than just at the top item and see other stuff that could be done to move the thing forward. Thus while we're waiting for the other thing to happen we can still make progress. Often too this has the nice side effect of putting pressure on the laggards to complete their stuff.

Example 5 Dealing with specialists

Doctors, lawyers and software people are probably the worst offenders, but many people do it. You know the kind of thing I mean – somebody takes the attitude that they know better than you and that you should just leave things to them. They talk (often condescendingly) to you in the technobabble of their particular discipline in the hope that it will baffle you into silence. If that doesn't work, and you actually question them, they continue to send over waves of technobabble to intimidate you into silence. Almost always too – particularly with lawyers and software people – there's a sense of, 'It'll take as long as it takes. Don't ask why – it just will.'

The truth is that doctors, lawyers and software people – indeed, all specialists – are as subject to the principle of sequences of events as the next person. With doctors, to hand your health or even your life over to someone like this is crazy. With lawyers, it is often your financial well-being that is at stake; and many of us these days are having to deal with software people. If you are in charge – which you are if you hire a doctor, hire a lawyer or are managing a software person – then among other things the onus is on them to tell you clearly and unambiguously what the sequence of events is.

Furthermore, you are entitled to question the sequence of events. This is particularly true of lawyers and software people. What happens next? What does what you just said mean? What does it translate into in simple language? Who is doing what? Why does it take this long? ('It just does' is not a good enough answer.) Why can't it be done quicker? What's the holdup? Explain to me in simple language who is doing what. What am I expected to do? Keep doing this until you get a clear picture in your mind of what is going on. Don't be afraid to make suggestions or offer improvements to the plan (i.e. the sequence of events). Once they get the hang of how the game is going to be played, they'll deliver a much better service for your (or your company's) money.

Example 6 Problem solving

We can use the three principles we've seen so far to come up with a method for problem solving. The first thing we need to know – and principle 2, know what you're trying to do, tells us this – is what exactly is the problem. Sometimes the stated issue is not the real issue; sometimes people phrase a problem by stating a solution; sometimes, even if a problem is stated correctly, by 'pulling back' and seeing the bigger picture we can solve the problem more completely. The 'understand what you're trying to do' tool will enable you to state the problem clearly.

Having identified the problem, it's useful to know what the ideal solution would be. Among other things, this will enable you to gauge the quality of any other solutions that emerge. The 'know if what you're trying to do is what everyone wants' tool in Chapter 2 is a way of figuring out the solution that would best meet the needs of all of the parties involved in the problem.

We know what problem we're trying to solve, we know what the ideal solution would be. Now, let's identify a range of possible solutions. Principle 3, there is always a sequence of events, enables us to do this. In particular, the 'there always has to be another way' tool enables us to find other solutions to the problem.

Finally, knowing the ideal solution, we pick from our range of possible solutions the one that comes closest to the ideal.

Example 7 Discussions that lead nowhere

Have you ever had one of those discussions that leads nowhere? I'm sure you know the kind of thing I mean. You and a colleague (or maybe several of them) have a discussion where you are entirely in agreement about something. 'Somebody really ought to do something' seems to be the unspoken subtext. However, at the end of the discussion, everyone walks away and nothing happens. (Actually, in my experience, whole meetings can often be conducted like this.)

Knowing that there is always a sequence of events can stop this from happening. If there is agreement on some issue, then for anything to happen, a sequence of events must flow from that agreement. Pointing this out and putting even one or two jobs in train (i.e. putting actions on people) ensures that whatever great idea was hatched during the discussion is not forgotten, but rather is acted upon.

AND SO, WHAT SHOULD YOU DO?

1 Keep a list of the things you're trying to do.

2 Update it regularly – every day, every week, whatever works for you.

3 Use principle 2 to understand new things as they come along. Then use the tools we have described in the 'Tools' section of this chapter to build sequences of events. Keep sequences of events in stacks and work the stacks as we have described.

4 Always look for action lists after meetings, phone calls and so on.

5 Use brainstorming to generate alternative ways forward and hence sequences of events.

6 Make bread in parallel with doing something else. Bread making is a classic example of a sequence of events. Making bread while doing one or more other things is a great way of practising doing many things at once, i.e. managing sequences of events.

7 Always try to have a plan (sequence of events) for a meeting, for a working day, for a project. It'll go so much more smoothly as a result. The next section – A little planning is better than a lot of firefighting – summarizes the common-sense way to build a plan. At the end of Chapter 4 there is a corresponding section which summarizes the common-sense way to execute a plan.

A little planning is better than a lot of firefighting

This section and the corresponding section at the end of Chapter 4 bring together many of the ideas in this book. These two sections tell you *everything* you need to do to plan and execute any project in a common-sense way, using the least amount of effort. The two sections describe a method with ten steps. Five of the steps are to do with building a plan for the project; the other five are to do with executing the plan. Not all of the steps are equally important and so there is a weighting attached to each of them. The weightings add up to 100 and, at any time over the life of your project, you can score your project out of 100. This score is something we call a Probability of Success Indicator or PSI. The PSI tells you how likely or not your project is to succeed. Low weightings will point you to the weak areas in your project i.e. those that you must fix if your project is to succeed. The steps and weightings are as follows:

Weighting	Step
	PLANNING THE PROJECT
20	1 Figure out the goal of the project
20	2 Make a list of jobs
10	3 The project must have one leader
10	4 Find people to do the work
10	5 (a) Put a margin for error in the plan
	(b) Manage people's expectations
	EXECUTING THE PLAN
10	6 Use an appropriate leadership style
10	7 Know what's going on
10	8 Tell people what's going on
0	9 Repeat steps 1 to 8 until the project is over
0	10 Do a post-mortem or review on the project

The five planning steps are described below; the five execution ones at the end of Chapter 4. There is a section for each step. Within each section, we present the step first – what it is, the ideas behind it – and then we tell you how to carry out that step.

1 Figure out the goal of the project

1.1 The idea

The biggest single reason why projects go wrong is that they were never possible in the first place. It is important to realize that when a project is given to you, you are also – almost invariably – given what we might call constraints or 'baggage'. Baggage comes in three forms:

- time – the project must be done by a certain date;
- money – the project must be done for a certain budget;
- resources – the project must be done with a certain group of people.

If you try both to plan the project realistically *and* to deal with the baggage at the same time, you will potentially get yourself in a lot of trouble. Therefore we do these two things separately. First we build a plan as if there were no baggage, using steps 1–4 and 5(a), and then we deal with the baggage in step 5(b).

To fix the goal of your project, you need to take account of three things:

1 You must establish a boundary around your project and say, 'These things within the boundary are part of my project and these things outside are not.'

2 Changes to the boundary will occur over the life of the project. When a change occurs on a project you have only three possible ways of dealing with it:

- it's a change control event (a significant change). Changes to the agreed project scope, changes to the agreed project resourcing or assumptions turning out not to be true all constitute change control events;
- use contingency;
- work more hours.

3 You must pick the right boundary, i.e. the one that keeps all of the stakeholders[1] in the project as happy as possible.

1.2 What to do

1 Identify the baggage and put it to one side for the moment.

2 Answer the question, 'How will I know when this project is over?' What point in time marks the end of this project? What is the final event that marks its conclusion? This will tell you the goal of the project.

3 Make a list of all the stakeholders. For each stakeholder, write down their 'win conditions', i.e. what they would regard as a successful project. (If you are in doubt, ask them.)

4 When you've done this, go to step 2.

2 Make a list of jobs

2.1 The idea

The single biggest problem in project management occurs here. The difficulty with this step is that you have to predict the future, something that nobody can do with 100 per cent certainty. The best you can hope for here is that the error in your prediction will be as small as possible.

There are two things you can do to help you. One is that you can record what happened on previous projects – how long particular

---

[1] A 'stakeholder' is any person or organization affected by the project.

tasks took, how much work was involved in them, what they cost – and use this information when you come to plan your next project. (This idea is discussed again in steps 7 and 10.)

The other is to put lots of *detail* in the plan. By breaking down the work to be done into small elements of detail, you are less likely to miss vital elements of the project.

One other important point that we need to clarify here is the difference between duration and work.

▨ **Duration**, sometimes also called Elapsed time, is *how long* a particular job is going to take. It is measured in the normal units of time – hours, days, months and so on. The duration of a soccer match, for example, is 90 minutes.

▨ **Work**, sometimes called Effort, is how much work is in a particular job. It is measured in units, like man-days, person-hours, person-years and so on. The work in a soccer match, if we count two teams of 11, a referee, two linesmen and a fourth official is 26 times 90 minutes, i.e. 39 person-hours.

Durations are important because they enable us to figure out *how long* all or part of a project will take. Efforts are important because they enable us to figure out *how much* all or part of a project will cost.

2.2 What to do

1 Involve the people who will do the project in figuring out the list of jobs. If they're not available, get somebody to help you. The worst thing you can do is to do this by yourself.

2 Identify the big pieces of work to be done in the project, the bits that get you from the start to the end. (Note that there are going to have to be chunks of work that ensure that each stakeholder's win condition gets met. Win conditions don't just get met by accident!)

3   Within each of these big pieces of work, identify the detailed jobs that have to be done.

4   Break everything down such that each job you identify is between 1 and 5 days' duration or 1 and 5 person-days of work.

5   Use cause and effect: each job causes/triggers further jobs. Use this idea to help you build sequences of jobs.

6   Be as specific and concrete as possible, i.e. rather than saying 'requirements gathering', say 'Charlie meets with the IT people for 2 days to explain his requirements'. Using simple language to describe jobs is a good way to ensure this. (Write it so that a child could understand it!)

7   Where you don't know something, make an assumption.

8   Store all the jobs in a work breakdown structure or WBS, i.e. show the project as being made up of the big pieces of work, which in turn are made up of the smaller pieces.

9   In step 2 we come up with four things:
   ▨ jobs;
   ▨ the dependencies between jobs;
   ▨ work;
   ▨ duration.

10 Go to step 3.

2.3 A note on the project budget

You can think of the budget as just an extra column after Work and Duration. We can work out the cost of (budget for) each job using two elements:

▨ labour – calculated by multiplying Work by Daily Rate;

▨ any other costs – equipment, travel and subsistence, software, etc.

Adding up all of these gives the total budget.

3 The project must have one leader

3.1 The idea

Your project must have one leader, one person who ensures that all the jobs identified in the previous step get done.

Project Manager is not just a title. It is a real job with real duties, and those duties involve doing whatever has to be done to ensure that all of the jobs identified in step 2 are completed.

Obviously, these duties can only be carried out if you set time aside to do them. A good rule of thumb is to take 10 per cent of the total effort (not duration) in your project, and add this on for project management.

3.2 What to do

1 Calculate 10 per cent of the total effort (not duration) in your project.

2 Put an additional job in your work breakdown structure called 'Project Management', with the amount of effort from (1).

3 Go to step 4.

4 Find people to do the work

4.1 The idea

Like many things in life, project management is a problem in supply and demand. The demand comes from the work to be done (identified in step 2); the supply comes here, in this step. Essentially, if there are 100 person-days' worth of work to be done, there are going to have to be 100 person-days' worth of people to do the work.

The problem arises, of course, because the demand (work to be done) has a tendency to go up ('Can we just have this one extra thing?' 'I thought that was already included' etc.) and the supply has a tendency to go down and down and down ('There are no resources available' 'We need Charlie for this other project' 'Sorry, I'm not going to be able to do that for another week' etc.).

Your job here is to ensure that there are people to do all the jobs and that those people have time available to carry them out.

4.2 What to do

1 Put *people's* names against all the jobs in your work break-down structure.

2 Find out how much each person is available to do each job. If a job is 10 person-days and Charlie is available 1 day per week, the job will last 10 weeks; if he's available full time it will last only 2 weeks – a huge difference.

3 Store all of the resulting information in a Gantt chart – a chart showing who does what when.

4 Go to step 5(a).

5(a) Put a margin for error in the plan

5(a).1 The idea

The plan that you've built as a result of applying steps 1–4 is your best prediction of how your project could unfold. In theory, at this point, you could deal with the baggage, but there's one other thing you must do before doing this. You must make the plan resilient by putting a margin for error in the plan. Without a margin for error, it's quite likely that your plan will fail the first time something unexpected happens on your project.

There are two ways to put a margin for error into the plan. One is to add in contingency. There are a number of ways to do this but in the section that follows we just describe one way. The other is to do risk analysis – attack the risks on your project before they attack you!

5(a).2 What to do

1 Add some additional time on to the end date of the project. This is to cover unexpected events that might occur over the life of the project. If you're looking for a rule of thumb then maybe add 15 per cent of the duration of the project. In other words, if the project lasts seven months, add an additional month for contingency.

2 Do a risk analysis of your project.
- Identify the risks to your project – those things that could cause the project to go wrong.
- Grade each risk as to how likely it is to happen. Use a scale of 1–3, where 1 = not very likely; 3 = highly likely; 2 = anything else.
- Grade each risk as to its impact if it does happen. Use the same 1–3 scale.
- Multiply Likelihood by Impact to give Exposure.
- For the high Exposure items (i.e. Exposure = 6 or 9), identify actions you can take to reduce these risks.
- Put these actions (i.e. jobs) into the plan and treat them just the same as any other jobs.

3 Go to step 5(b).

5(b) Manage people's expectations

5(b).1 The idea

A successful project is one where the stakeholders' expectations are set initially and then managed over the life of the project. To put it another way, your project will be successful if your project stakeholders always know how they stand.

A major part of this is setting the stakeholders' expectations initially, and that involves dealing with whatever baggage may have come with the project. The next section tells you what to do.

5(b).2 What to do

1 It may be that the dates, resource levels and budgets in your plan meet the constraints imposed by the baggage. In that case you can make commitments to the stakeholders based on your plan, i.e. you can tell them the end date, what the project will cost and what resources you need.

2 If (1) doesn't happen – and it rarely does! – then you can do the following. The version of the plan you have may not satisfy the constraints. But a revised version might. There are four variables connected with the plan that you can vary. These are:

- what the project is delivering;
- the delivery date;
- the work involved / the budget;
- the quality of what's being delivered.

By varying one or more of these it may be possible to come up with a version of the plan that satisfies the stakeholders.

3 If (2) doesn't happen, it means the stakeholders are asking for something that is impossible. *You should always decline impossible missions.* Insist that the stakeholders only deal in reality, i.e. engage in (2) preceding. The stakeholders may not all be overjoyed at the end of the negotiation, but at least they know they can rely on what's being committed to, rather than being promised something which – in the fullness of time – turns out to have been impossible to do.

4 Now you're ready to begin executing the project.

04

Things don't get done if people don't do them

This chapter makes the rather obvious point that things won't be done if people don't do them. In particular, things won't get done if people don't have the time to do them.

Questions

For answers to Questions, please see Answers to questions and scores on page 185.

Q.1 You're involved in a 'rescue' of a project or venture. In other words, it's all gone horribly wrong and you've been called in to clean up the mess. You discover there is a plan, and the plan is actually current, i.e. it has been updated recently. The plan has a well-defined goal, which has stayed relatively stable, and what looks like a comprehensive list of jobs (sequence of events). In looking at the plan you find that lots of the jobs – particularly those that were meant to be finished a long time ago – have phrases such as 'New hire', 'TBD', 'A N Other' against them, i.e. generic names rather than real people's names.

(a) Is this the main reason why the venture went wrong?

(b) Is it something else?

(c) Is it too soon to say? Must you go and gather loads more information about the status of the project?

(d) Is it nothing to do with the project but actually to do with technical issues involved in the venture?

Q.2 Bozo (it's just a name – it doesn't imply any reflection on his character or ability) shows up from central casting to work for you. He says he's available 'full time'. If this is true, i.e. if he genuinely has no other things to work on, and you discount vacation and public holidays, how many real days of his time are you getting in a working week? Is it:

(a) 3.75 days?

(b) Closer to (but greater than) 4 days?

(c) 2.5 days?

(d) Nearly 5 days?

Q.3 You're ready to begin a new venture with the merry band of brothers (and sisters) that you've chosen ('handpicked'!), inherited or otherwise acquired. Of the following, which is most likely to sink your venture?

(a) Poor salaries.

(b) Poor working conditions.

(c) Not playing to people's strengths.

(d) Poor management by you.

The idea

Once you've figured out what it is you're trying to do (principle 2, know what you're trying to do) and what needs to happen to get it done (principle 3, there is always a sequence of events), the next thing is to get the things done. That is what this chapter is all about. But first a story.

A couple of years ago, my ex-wife's nephew spent a few weeks in our company on work experience from school. Shortly after he started with us, I was chatting with him and he asked, 'What exactly do you do here?' I explained that we were a project management company. We sold our services to high-tech and knowledge industries. We did training, we did consulting, we ran projects for clients. He asked about the training course. 'What kinds of things do you teach them?' 'Oh,' I said, 'for example, we teach that if you have a big job to do, you break it up into lots of smaller jobs.' He seemed happy enough with that for openers. 'So what else?' he asked. 'Well, we teach them that jobs don't get done if people don't do them.' At this he smiled. 'You teach this to adults?' he asked. I nodded. 'Do you charge a lot for this?' he asked. 'It's not cheap,' I replied. His smile broadened and he began to shake his head. 'I'd better go back to work,' he said.

It's so sickeningly obvious, and yet jobs *don't* get done if people don't do them, and if enough jobs don't get done, then things go awry, sometimes badly so. In general, people don't maliciously set out not to do things. But there is a variety of reasons why it can happen. The most obvious ones are:

- confusion – they didn't know they were meant to do something or precisely what it was they were meant to do;

- over-commitment – they knew they were meant to do it but they didn't have the time;

- inability – they didn't have the expertise, experience or training to do the job.

So if we are to address the problem of people not doing certain things, our tools must tackle these three killers. We introduce the tools in the next section. They are:

- make sure every job has somebody to do it. This should deal with individual confusion;

- dance cards – to deal, first of all, with over-commitment but also with confusion within an organization;

- maximizing the strengths of the team. This should deal with inability;

- the strip board, which will tackle all three in one swell foop!

Tools

Make sure every job has somebody to do it

Our first tool is a pretty straightforward one. We just want to make sure that at the end of a meeting, a phone call, at the start of a project or venture, we know who has to do what. I'll fully accept that at the beginning of a venture we may not know who's going to work on what. They may not have been identified, assigned or hired. So it is perfectly valid for us to have certain jobs in our sequences of events where nobody has been identified to do them. Then it is fine if we put in 'generic' names such as 'Marketing person' or 'Engineer' or 'Designer' or even the dreaded 'TBDs' and 'New hires' and 'A N Others'.

But *some time before that event is due to happen,* there had better be a warm, living, loving human being in place who is actually going to get the job done.

Dance cards

You may not have necessarily thought of things in this way before, but much of life is a problem in supply and demand. Money. We don't have enough money (supply) to do all the things we'd like to do (demand). Or we have a business and it is successful – revenue (supply) exceeds costs (demand). Or, heaven forbid, our business is unsuccessful because revenue (supply) is less than costs (demand). Or, thinking about resources, we (as a department, division, organization, company) are trying to do too much with too few people or too little equipment. Or, thinking in terms of time, there never seem to be enough hours in the day (supply) to do all the things we want to do, have to do or have committed to do (demand).

"Much of life is a problem in supply and demand."

A dance card is a way of investigating *time* from a supply and demand point of view. Just to get it out of the way, the term 'dance card' is a reference to those more genteel days when ladies went to dances and had a dance card showing the (fixed number of) dances that were available that night. Then, if a gentleman wanted to dance with them, he wrote his name against a particular dance – a waltz or a tango or whatever. Thus that time slot was booked, if you want to think of it that way, and so could not be booked by anybody else.

I hope you can see the analogy. You have a certain amount of time (or time slots) available every day, every week, every month, every year. In work, at home or wherever, certain slots get booked by other people – your boss, your customer, people who work for you, your children, your wife, husband, boyfriend, girlfriend and so on. Given that in general, there will be more demand on your time than you will be able to satisfy, how can you ensure that you put time into the right things? The dance card, which we will describe shortly, is a tool for doing just that. It also has other uses, but let's see first what a dance card looks like (see Figure 4.1).

I'm sure you can see that it looks suspiciously like it was made using a spreadsheet. The leftmost column lists all the things in which the dance card's owner is involved. The next two columns indicate how much work is estimated to go into these things over the period under investigation. Days per month (dpm), days per week (dpw), hours per day or just plain days are all good ways of estimating how much work needs to be done. The remaining columns show how this work will be spread out over the period under investigation – in this case, eight months. There are two other items of interest. The top row shows how many days are available per month and also the total number of days available (160) over the period. (Note that rather than trying to allow for the different numbers of working days in different countries, we have assumed that every month consists of 20 days. You could adjust this up or down for your own situation. For example, in Europe, December is definitely not 20 working days in most companies.) The other item of interest is the total of all the work this dance card owner has to do – in this example, 289 days.

Now here the owner has some problems to address – that's if you'd call having twice as much work to do as time available to do it a problem, which I believe I would. We will look at how one might address such a problem in one of the examples which follows. I hope, though, you can see that the dance card is a good tool for understanding the sources of over-commitment, at least to begin with. As it turns out, it is also the tool to begin fixing those problems, but we will see this shortly. And happily, there is at least one other use we can put it to, which we will also see in the examples.

Figure 4.1 A dance card

Total days available:	160		20	20	20	20	20	20	20	20
# Project	Basis	Total	Nov	Dec	Jan	Feb	Mar	Apr	May	Jun
1 Project Abel	25 days	25	2.5	2.5	2.5	3.5	3.5	3.5	3.5	3.5
2 Project Baker	25 days	25	2.5	2.5	2.5	3.5	3.5	3.5	3.5	3.5
3 Project Charlie	2 dpm	16	2	2	2	2	2	2	2	2
4 Project Dog	1 dpw	40	5	5	5	5	5	5	5	5
5 E-mail	8 dpm	64	8	8	8	8	8	8	8	8
6 Training other people	1 dpm	8	1	1	1	1	1	1	1	1
7 Recruitment	1 dpm	8	1	1	1	1	1	1	1	1
8 Project Easy	10 days	10	2	2	1	1	1	1	1	1
9 Holidays	5 days	5		5						
10 Meetings	2.5 dpw	80	10	10	10	10	10	10	10	10
11 Training courses	2 days	2	0.5	0.5	1					
12 Trips	2 days	2			2					
13 Conference calls	0.5 dpm	4	0.5	0.5	0.5	0.5	0.5	0.5	0.5	0.5
Total days work to do:		289	35.0	40.0	36.5	35.5	35.5	35.5	35.5	35.5

Maximizing the strengths of the team

One of the most foolish assumptions we could make would be to assume that just because we've got our sequence of events and we've given each job to some member of our motley crew, it's all going to happen. Apart from the reasons already identified – confusion or over-commitment – there is the question of expertise and ability. Looking at it somewhat more broadly or holistically, we can think of it like this: given that everybody has strengths and weaknesses, how can we ensure that we use as many of the strengths as possible and reduce as much as possible the effects of the weaknesses?

Whole rainforests have been destroyed to provide the paper for the books, MBA theses and all the rest of the things that have been written in relation to this. In keeping with our philosophy of finding a simple solution (principle 1, many things are simple) however, the following is a method that I have used and found to be both useful and effective.

For each job allocated to a person, rate that allocation according to the following scheme.

1 **Superstar**. The person likes to do that particular job, has all the necessary skills and will almost certainly deliver.

2 **Solid citizen**. The person is happy enough to do the job and knows how to do it. Maybe they don't get particularly fired up about doing it, but there's a pretty good chance they'll deliver.

3 **Dodgy**. For whatever reason – lack of motivation, lack of expertise, lack of time – there's a good chance this one isn't going to happen.

4 **Trainee**. They're new to whatever it is. They're going to need hand-holding, nurturing, mentoring, coaching, formal training, micro-management before we can be confident they'll deliver.

5 Goner. It isn't going to happen. You need to find some other way of getting this job done.

Now, we can make a few observations about this scheme. The first is, how do we know that a person falls into a particular category if we've never worked with them before? Simple. Give them a few jobs from the sequence of events and see how they do. After two or three deliveries or non-deliveries, we'll have a much clearer idea.

Next, who should decide who falls into a particular category? Two possibilities. You can decide and act accordingly. Alternatively – and this is better, but maybe harder to do – you and the person can rate their capabilities on particular jobs. Then you compare notes and you (both) see where you might have not estimated the person's ability to deliver correctly.

Finally, what do the classifications mean for you? The main thing is that you will manage the different situations differently. For example, you wouldn't manage a superstar the same way you would a trainee. In fact, the following are the leadership or management styles that would seem most appropriate in the different situations.

1 Superstar. Leave them to get on with it with minimal sticking your nose in.

2 Solid citizen. Don't get too much in their way, but neither assume it's all just going to happen.

3 Dodgy. Establish as quickly as you can – by giving them a few jobs from the sequence of events and seeing the result – whether it's going to happen or not. If it is, it becomes a 2 – solid citizen; if not, it becomes a 5 – goner.

4 Trainee. Do all of what we said in the previous list to ensure you make them into at least a 2 – solid citizen.

5 Goner. You need to deal with the person. Your choices are anything on the spectrum from firing to rehabilitation.

Figure 4.2 A section of a strip board

Day #	Date	Cast [jobs]							
		Bilbo	**Frodo**	**Sam**	**Senior Designer**	**Aragorn**	**Gandalf**	**Barliman**	**Underhill**
1	4-Sep-00			Design styling					
2	5-Sep-00	Plan	Arrange meet	Design styling					
3	6-Sep-00			Design styling					
4	7-Sep-00			Design styling					
5	8-Sep-00			Agree site map with client & get design reqs					
6	9-Sep-00								
7	10-Sep-00								
8	11-Sep-00			Concept development					
9	12-Sep-00			Interface development					
10	13-Sep-00			Internal design review					
11	14-Sep-00			Client design presentation	Client design presentation				
12	15-Sep-00			Client-driven changes					
13	16-Sep-00								
14	17-Sep-00								
15	18-Sep-00			Present design and get sign-off	Present design and get sign-off				
16	19-Sep-00			Section thread design	Section thread design				
17	20-Sep-00			Section thread design	Section thread design				
18	21-Sep-00			Section thread design				Return final copy	
19	22-Sep-00			Present to client				Present to client	
20	23-Sep-00								
21	24-Sep-00								
22	25-Sep-00			Main site production	Main site production				
23	26-Sep-00			Main site production	Main site production				
24	27-Sep-00			Main site production	Main site production				
25	28-Sep-00			Main site production	Main site production				
26	29-Sep-00			Main site production	Main site production				
27	30-Sep-00								
28	1-Oct-00								
29	2-Oct-00			Main site production	Main site production				

No	Date				
30	3-Oct-00		Main site production	Main site production	
31	4-Oct-00		Main site production	Main site production	
32	5-Oct-00		Main site production	Main site production	
33	6-Oct-00		Main site production	Main site production	
34	**7-Oct-00**				
35	**8-Oct-00**				Review work to date
36	9-Oct-00			Upload to dev	
37	10-Oct-00			Integration; making changes to site	
38	11-Oct-00			Integration; making changes to site	
39	12-Oct-00			Integration; making changes to site	
40	13-Oct-00			Integration; review work to date	
41	**14-Oct-00**				
42	**15-Oct-00**				
43	16-Oct-00			Integration, making changes to site	
44	17-Oct-00		QA	QA	
45	18-Oct-00		QA	QA	
46	19-Oct-00		QA	QA	
47	20-Oct-00			Insert metatags and keywords; supply demo version for pilot	Site review and sign-off
48	**21-Oct-00**				
49	**22-Oct-00**				
50	23-Oct-00	Main site production / in Main site production / integration/QA			
51	24-Oct-00	Main site production / in Main site production / integration/QA			
52	25-Oct-00	Main site production / in Main site production / integration/QA			
53	26-Oct-00	Main site production / in Main site production / integration/QA			
54	27-Oct-00	Main site production / in Main site production / integration/QA			
55	**28-Oct-00**				
56	**29-Oct-00**				
57	**30-Oct-00**				
58	31-Oct-00	Main site production / in Main site production / integration/QA			
56	23-Oct-00				
57	24-Oct-00				
58	25-Oct-00				
59	26-Oct-00				
60	27-Oct-00				

The strip board

The strip board is a simple, elegant and immensely powerful tool taken from the film-making industry. Its purpose is to show exactly who is doing exactly what exactly when. You may argue that tools like Gantt charts (particularly if they're generated with fancy software packages such as Microsoft Project) do precisely this. I will argue in return that they do it with nothing like the accuracy, ease of use or visibility of a strip board.

An example of a section of a strip board is shown in Figure 4.2 on the previous page. You will find an example of its use on pages 83–5.

Examples

Example 1 Getting a life (Part 1)

One of the biggest problems in the developed world today is that of creating a balance between life and work. We work to live, yet if work takes up all our time, we have no life. Studies, articles and books on this subject are starting to appear with increasing frequency. And we probably don't need studies to tell us that this has become a problem for us. More and more time spent getting to and from work; increasing pressures piled on to us at work ('if you don't do it, I'll find somebody who can'); bringing work home with us – all of these things mean that our life is gradually being eroded by our work.

It is possible to stop this rot. I say this from experience – as someone who rarely works more than 40 hours a week. To do so, you need three things. First, you need some kind of tool or measuring device to see how well or how badly you're doing. We've already seen this tool – it's the dance card. Next, you need to take on board principle 4, that things don't get done if people don't do them. From this flows the notion that things don't get done if people don't have the time to do them. Thus we must find ways to make the time available so that the right things get done. Finally – and this is the magic ingredient – you need the willpower to make this happen. If you really want to do it, it will happen. But you must *really really* want to do it.

Let's take the dance card from Figure 4.1, give to it a character we shall affectionately call Bozo, and reproduce it here as Figure 4.3 (overleaf).

It doesn't take a rocket scientist to see that Bozo is a potential candidate for Burn-out City. Even if he only began working this hard today – an unlikely assumption – his dance card shows that he has twice as much work to do as time available to do it. He is not in a situation where he has only a 'hump' to clear, and which once cleared, he would be OK: Bozo isn't on a hump, he's on a plateau. On this plateau, as far as he can see off into the future, quite literally as long as he stays in that job, he has twice as much work to do as he has time available to do it. And that is not all. Unless he does something about this, then (a) it will never get better and (b) it can only get worse. This is Bozo's starting point. It is because of this gloomy prognosis that he decides to do something about it. Maybe the fact that his children didn't recognize him recently and his wife thinks she has a lodger rather than a husband also spurs him on to try to resolve the problem.

There are only two things Bozo can do to fix this supply–demand problem. He can increase the supply or decrease the demand. Increasing the supply means making more hours available, hours that he will have to take out of his personal life. Bozo decides that this is no longer an option for him.

If he is not going to increase supply, then he must decrease demand – that is, he must find ways of doing less work. (Best to call a spade a spade here.) There are three ways he can do this:

■ find smarter ways to do particular things, for example he might be able to delegate;

Figure 4.3 **Bozo's dance card**

Total days available:	160			20	20	20	20	20	20	20	20
#	Project	Basis	Total	Nov	Dec	Jan	Feb	Mar	Apr	May	Jun
1	Project Abel	25 days	25	2.5	2.5	2.5	3.5	3.5	3.5	3.5	3.5
2	Project Baker	25 days	25	2.5	2.5	2.5	3.5	3.5	3.5	3.5	3.5
3	Project Charlie	2 dpm	16	2	2	2	2	2	2	2	2
4	Project Dog	1 dpw	40	5	5	5	5	5	5	5	5
5	E-mail (2 days per week)	8 dpm	64	8	8	8	8	8	8	8	8
6	Training other people	1 dpm	8	1	1	1	1	1	1	1	1
7	Recruitment	1 dpm	8	1	1	1	1	1	1	1	1
8	Project Easy	10 days	10	2	2	2	1	1	1	1	1
9	Holidays	5 days	5		5						
10	Meetings	2.5 dpw	80	10	10	10	10	10	10	10	10
11	Training courses	2 days	2	0.5	0.5	1					
12	Trips	2 days	2			2					
13	Conference calls	0.5 dpm	4	0.5	0.5	0.5	0.5	0.5	0.5	0.5	0.5
	Total days work to do:	289		35.0	40.0	36.5	35.5	35.5	35.5	35.5	35.5
	Overload:	81%									

- don't do particular things in the period under investigation;
- don't do particular things at all.

We will approach this problem with a series of 'interventions' (as a doctor might say), starting with those which are easy to implement and building up to much more radical ones. You can go straight to the radical ones if you prefer, but a gentler slope upwards might suit you better.

OK, let's begin. We're going to explore some 'work smarter' things. When somebody's personal supply–demand is as out of whack as Bozo's is, it is pointless looking at the things that consume small amounts of his time, for example 'training courses' (2 days) or 'trips' (2 days). We need to look at the big hitters such as 'meetings' (80 days) or 'e-mail' (64 days). (Note that 'e-mail' can be taken to include all forms of stuff arriving in Bozo's inbox, including those normal 'interruptions' that are part of any working day.) We discover, from talking to Bozo, that he deals with every interruption when it comes in. In essence, he tries to operate an empty-at-all-times inbox. Our first job is to wean him off this habit.

"We're going to explore some 'work smarter' things."

We suggest to him that instead of doing this he should limit himself to checking his inbox twice a day, once in the morning and once in the afternoon, for an hour each time. Also he should turn off the e-mail notification on his computer. Two hours a day is 10 hours a week, i.e. 1.25 days per week instead of 2 days per week as he has at the moment. By this simple stratagem he saves 0.75 days per week, which is 3 days per month (assuming 4 weeks in a month) which is 24 days over the period. Such a change in Bozo's behaviour is unlikely to go unnoticed for too long. Sooner or later, somebody will say to him, 'Didn't you read my e-mail?' To which he should explain that he now only reads his e-mail twice a day, from, say, 9:00 to 10:00 and 2:00 to 3:00. This is useful information (not to mention a useful tip) for his colleague, and the issue should end there. Bozo is now ready for the next dose of medicine, which is a bit heavier.

There are two alternative treatments at this point. One would be to reduce the twice a day to once a day. This would halve the 24 days for e-mail to 12 days. However, it has to be said that hard-core e-mail junkies find this difficult to do. So an alternative – and happily, it's even more effective – is to do the following. Twice a day, as we have described, sweep your e-mail. This time, however, rather than spending an hour on it, just deal with those ones that are 'glowing red', i.e. they *have* to be done today. Everything else, leave it. Bozo does this, tentatively at first, and then more confidently and finally, religiously, i.e. he is brutal as to what *has* to be done today. The result is that he reduces his time spent on e-mail/inbox/interruptions to no more than 1 day per week, i.e. 4 days per month, i.e. 32 days in the period under investigation. Bozo's colleagues will merely notice that Bozo has become somewhat less tolerant of (relatively) unimportant interruptions and issues. Or to put it another way, Bozo deals only with things which are important.

Now, it turns out that there are even more radical things he can do. If you remember, Bozo's original philosophy amounted to 'check everything that comes in, in case there's something important, and try to keep a clear inbox'. A different approach would be to say, 'If something is important enough I need to find out about it and not worry about the rest of the stuff in the inbox.' To implement this, you could take the following approach. Check your inbox once a day, or you could even (gasp!) go to Monday/Wednesday/Friday or even (bigger gasp!) Monday and Friday. If something is important and urgent/has to be done today/glowing red, do it. Otherwise just leave it to rot in your inbox. When your inbox is full, empty it, either by going through it item by item or, better still, trash the lot and start again. Will you have missed something important? Well, why don't you do it and see what happens. If you did miss something important, you can do your inbox sweeping more often. If you didn't, you could consider doing it even less often (gasp again!).

Getting back to Bozo, his dance card now looks like Figure 4.4 overleaf.

If you try these techniques, you will find that they will have the same effect. You may fall by the wayside at first, but if you persevere and make these simple procedures part of your working day, you will find that you save a lot of time. Also, it will make you confident enough about your ability to change your behaviours that you may be prepared to try the next batch of medicine, which is a bit more severe. By the same token, if you haven't mastered the techniques we have just described, it is unlikely that you'll have the stomach for what follows.

Example 2 Getting a life (Part 2)

Let's return to Bozo. As we said in the previous example, we still haven't begun to administer the really heavy medicine. At 61 per cent overload, Bozo is still in an unhealthy position. Let's assume that he has no further options under the 'work smarter' heading. There is nobody to whom he can delegate anything. The 'meetings' and 'conference calls', both of which consume an extraordinary amount of his time, are all short, necessary events (because of the nature of his job). So neither the meetings nor the conference calls could be tightened up with good agendas, decent chairing and action items.

It's time to look at our two other approaches to reducing demand. If you remember, they were:

■ don't do particular things in the period under investigation;
■ don't do particular things at all.

Figure 4.4 Bozo's dance card with e-mail sorted

Total days available:	160		20	20	20	20	20	20	20	20
# Project	Basis	Total	Nov	Dec	Jan	Feb	Mar	Apr	May	Jun
1 Project Abel	25 days	25	2.5	2.5	2.5	3.5	3.5	3.5	3.5	3.5
2 Project Baker	25 days	25	2.5	2.5	2.5	3.5	3.5	3.5	3.5	3.5
3 Project Charlie	2 dpm	16	2	2	2	2	2	2	2	2
4 Project Dog	1 dpw	40	5	5	5	5	5	5	5	5
5 E-mail (1 day per week)	4 dpm	32	4	4	4	4	4	4	4	4
6 Training other people	1 dpm	8	1	1	1	1	1	1	1	1
7 Recruitment	1 dpm	8	1	1	1	1	1	1	1	1
8 Project Easy	10 days	10	2	2	1	1	1	1	1	1
9 Holidays	5 days	5		5						
10 Meetings	2.5 dpw	80	10	10	10	10	10	10	10	10
11 Training courses	2 days	2	0.5	0.5	1					
12 Trips	2 days	2			2					
13 Conference calls	0.5 dpm	4	0.5	0.5	0.5	0.5	0.5	0.5	0.5	0.5
Total days work to do:	257		31.0	36.0	32.5	31.5	31.5	31.5	31.5	31.5
Overload:	61%									

There is one way we could automatically balance the supply and demand in Bozo's dance card – if Bozo were to prioritize the items in his dance card and we simply made a cut at the point where he ran out of supply, the problem would be solved (at least from the numbers point of view). Without prejudging whether or not this would be a good thing to do, let's prioritize the items on Bozo's dance card. We'll use the 'what if we could only do one thing' test that we described earlier. After a lot of agonizing on Bozo's part, let's assume the result is as in Figure 4.5 overleaf.

The extra column we have added shows that, in theory at least, he should really only do his first five priorities and stop after that. I should say at this point that this is a valid suggestion and should not be dismissed out of hand. I'll agree that it's very strong medicine, but if you have the stomach for it, it solves the problem.

Let's assume, however, that this is much too radical a thing to do. So where do we go from here? An important factor that we haven't considered so far is what Bozo's performance is being measured on. Do we know which of the items in his list will become the basis for his performance appraisal or evaluation? Let's assume they're as shown in Figure 4.6 overleaf. (Note that we've grouped the key performance areas. Also, while Bozo's boss might not regard Bozo's holiday as a key performance area, Bozo does!)

What are we to make of this picture? And what realistic actions can we take as a result? This is where it's going to get tough for Bozo. Whichever way you look at this, Bozo is overworked. There are then two possibilities. Either this is a 'hump' or it isn't. It is a hump if some of Bozo's projects will end. Let's say, for example, that projects Dog, Abel and Baker will all be completed by the end of June. With these gone, Bozo's workload would drop to 167 days and, *provided he didn't take on anything*

Figure 4.5 Bozo's prioritized dance card

Total days available:	160				20	20	20	20	20	20	20	20
# Project	Basis	Total	Cumulative		Nov	Dec	Jan	Feb	Mar	Apr	May	Jun
1 Project Dog	1 dpw	40	40		5	5	5	5	5	5	5	5
2 Project Abel	25 days	25	65		2.5	2.5	2.5	3.5	3.5	3.5	3.5	3.5
3 Project Baker	25 days	25	90		2.5	2.5	2.5	3.5	3.5	3.5	3.5	3.5
4 Project Charlie	2 dpm	16	106		2	2	2	2	2	2	2	2
5 Meetings	2.5 dpw	80	186		10	10	10	10	10	10	10	10
6 E-mail (1 day per week)	4 dpm	32	218		4	4	4	4	4	4	4	4
7 Conference calls	0.5 dpm	4	222		0.5	0.5	0.5	0.5	0.5	0.5	0.5	0.5
8 Project Easy	10 days	10	232		2	2	1	1	1	1	1	1
9 Holidays	5 days	5	237			5						
10 Training courses	2 days	2	239		0.5	0.5	1					
11 Recruitment	1 dpm	8	247		1	1	1	1	1	1	1	1
12 Training other people	1 dpm	8	255		1	1	1	1	1	1	1	1
13 Trips	2 days	2	257				2					
Total days work to do:	**257**				**31.0**	**36.0**	**32.5**	**31.5**	**31.5**	**31.5**	**31.5**	**31.5**
Overload:	**61%**											

Figure 4.6 Bozo's prioritized dance card showing key performance areas

#	Key performance area	Project	Basis	Total	Cumulative	20 Nov	20 Dec	20 Jan	20 Feb	20 Mar	20 Apr	20 May	20 Jun
		Total days available:	160										
1	Yes	Project Dog	1 dpw	40	40	5	5	5	5	5	5	5	5
2	Yes	Project Abel	25 days	25	65	2.5	2.5	2.5	3.5	3.5	3.5	3.5	3.5
3	Yes	Project Baker	25 days	25	90	2.5	2.5	2.5	3.5	3.5	3.5	3.5	3.5
4	Yes	Project Charlie	2 dpm	16	106	2	2	2	2	2	2	2	2
5	Yes	Meetings	2.5 dpw	80	186	10	10	10	10	10	10	10	10
6	Yes	Project Easy	10 days	10	196	2	2	1	1	1	1	1	1
7	Yes	Training courses	2 days	2	198	0.5	0.5	1					
8	Yes	Recruitment	1 dpm	8	206	1	1	1	1	1	1	1	1
9	Yes	Training other people	1 dpm	8	214	1	1	1	1	1	1	1	1
10	Yes	Holidays	5 days	5	219		5						
11		E-mail (1 day per week)	4 dpm	32	251	4	4	4	4	4	4	4	4
12		Conference calls	0.5 dpm	4	255	0.5	0.5	0.5	0.5	0.5	0.5	0.5	0.5
13		Trips	2 days	2	257			2					
		Total days work to do:	257			31.0	36.0	32.5	31.5	31.5	31.5	31.5	31.5
		Overload:	61%										

new, he'd be in business. The other possibility – that this is not a hump – simply means that Bozo is doing the work of more than one person. This is not a tenable situation in the long term.

I hope you can see that in both cases, the problem facing Bozo is essentially the same. He must convince his boss that, in the first case, he cannot take on any/much new work when the current hump is cleared, and in the second case, he needs to shed some work. He must do a sales job. How will he do this?

To sell his boss on either of these notions, I think you'll agree there must be something in it for his boss. That magic ingredient can be deduced from the principle we have been describing in this chapter, namely that jobs don't get done if people don't do them. Bozo's approach to his boss uses this as its jumping-off point. It goes something like this.

If Bozo's dance card is as shown in Figure 4.6, he does not have enough time to do all of the things he is meant to do and upon which he will be measured. 'Continuous or extended overtime is not the answer,' Bozo states. 'Says who?' his boss replies, using that if-it's-good-enough-for-me-it's-good-enough-for-everyone-else tone of voice. 'Says him,' says Bozo, throwing on the table a copy of *The Deadline* by Tom DeMarco. In Chapter 15, under the heading 'The effects of pressure', it says some scary things.

- People under pressure don't think any faster.
- Extended overtime is a productivity reduction tactic.
- Short bursts of pressure and even overtime may be useful tactics as they focus people and increase the sense that the work is important, but extended pressure is always a mistake.
- Perhaps managers make so much use of pressure because they don't know what else to do, or are daunted by how difficult the alternatives are.
- Terrible suspicion: the real reason for use of pressure and

overtime may be to make everyone look better when the project fails.

(Bozo particularly enjoys saying the last two to his boss.)

'So who's he anyway?' the boss perhaps replies. But then Bozo goes at it from another angle. 'When I'm overloaded like this, I'm like a gladiator,' he says. 'Each time I go out in the arena I may succeed in surviving. But sooner or later, I'm going to fail. And when I fail, you fail. This is inevitable as long as I stay at this level of overload.'

'If, however, I can get back to an acceptable level, then in return I can *guarantee* you that I will *always* be able to deliver on my commitments. Which would you like? The uncertainty of a gladiator or the certainty of somebody who always delivers?' (Bozo needs to have defined what an acceptable level is. It might be, for example, that he has decided that *maximum* 50-hour weeks would be an acceptable level to work at. This would be an overload level of at most 25 per cent, representing a demand target in the range of 160–200 days, i.e. 160 days plus 25 per cent).

It might be that Bozo wins the argument at this point, that the sales job is done. What is perhaps more likely, though, is that the boss isn't buying. This is when Bozo's will to succeed in his quest to get a life will be tested to the limit. You see, the nice thing about all of this is that logic is on Bozo's side. Jobs *don't* get done if people don't do them. Bozo has the proof positive, in his dance card, that there are certain things upon which his performance is being measured that he has little or no chance of achieving. In the example in Figure 4.6, given that e-mails and conference calls must both be done in addition to the key performance areas, and that all projects are ongoing for the next eight months, Bozo has to lose two projects, say Abel and Baker. If he could do this, he would be down to 207 days, which would be round about the 25 per cent overload level we spoke of earlier.

So now he must take the bold step of saying to the powers that be, 'You'll have to find some other way of doing this. I can't do it.' They will bluster, of course, and behave like the Beadle when Oliver Twist asked for some more, but there's nothing they can do if Bozo holds firm. Again it may be that you feel this medicine is too strong for you. In that case you can go for the milder but no less effective version – it just takes longer to take effect – that you will endure whatever you have at the moment until those things end, but you won't take on any new things. And your justification for refusing things each time they are offered will be that you are already overloaded.

You have to understand that people will continue to throw stuff over the wall to you if you let them. In general they do this because they have no reason to believe there's a problem. *You haven't told them there's a problem.* If you don't tell them, there's no reason they should know; if you do tell them, they must find other ways to solve it. Productivity reduction tactics make no sense. Understand what a productivity reduction tactic actually is. It says that you will work long, stressful hours and you will *achieve less than if you had worked a straight 40-hour week.* Such a thing makes no sense whatsoever. Not for you, not for your customer, not for your employer, your boss, your company, your division, your department, your organization, not for anybody.

This is the true test of Bozo's moral fibre. Hold firm and eventually they must back down. Appear to sway, show any weakness, and they will assume, and rightly so, that you have agreed to return to the old patterns of behaviour. But if you hold firm you will be the winner. I say this both from experience and from having seen other people succeed at it. Jobs don't get done if people don't do them. It all flows from this.

Finally, there are three other things that may help you. First, read Example 5 later in this chapter. It talks about a situation where the organization is trying to do too much with too few resources. It may be that the problem of which you are the victim may have to be solved at an organizational level rather than an individual one.

Second, in Example 13 in Chapter 7, we describe a negotiation method where, rather than the negotiation being some kind of argument, it becomes a problem-solving session. The two sides have a mutual problem – in this case, you're working too hard and your boss needs to get many things done – and you try to find creative ways to ease *both* of your pains. The important thing in this negotiation method is that any solution you come up with has to be assessable on some objective basis. Dance cards provide you with a way of assessing the various solutions objectively. For example, you might want to ensure that you share some of the pain with your boss, that you're not the only one who gets to ease their overload situation.

Third, if you want to read a fictionalized account of somebody winning one of these negotiations in trying circumstances, you could read the worked example sections of my *How to Run Successful Projects in Web Time*.

Example 3 Aligning goals or objectives

One of the problems that occurs a lot in business is when you have, say, a bunch of people working for you (in a project or in a department, for example) and what they do is not what you expect. This can be bad for a couple of reasons. First of all, clearly, you didn't get to where you expected to be. Second, and often more importantly, you don't find this out until much too late.

A lot of ways have been devised to try to address this situation – management by objectives, sometimes involving almost lawyer-like definition of objectives, balanced score cards, key performance indicators, to name but a few. In my experience, dance cards represent a far better way to go about this. Here's how you do it.

1 Get each of the people who work for you to do a dance card to cover the period you're interested in.

2 Now go through the dance card with each person in turn, line by line.

3 Understand what they're intending to do over the period.

4 Look at the supply and demand and see how realistic the proposal is. (Hint: If they're as overloaded as Bozo was in the last example – even the Bozo of Figure 4.6 – there's a fair chance that the things they're proposing to do won't happen. While there's no fun in finding this out, better to find it out now than down the line. Note, too, that from the point of view of you as a manager, this approach is a far more sensible, civilized and effective way of dealing with supply–demand problems than the adversarial approach described in the preceding example.)

5 Correct any things that don't line up with your expectations so that you get a final dance card agreed by both parties that has a reasonable supply–demand balance.

6 Now let them loose, and you can be much more confident that their contribution to your success will be the one you wanted.

Example 4 Ensuring a project or endeavour gets done

It seems to me that there is a view in much of the business world that when you undertake something new, you do whatever planning you can, and after that it's in the lap of the gods. In fact, increasingly these days, there seems to be a tendency to say, 'We don't have time to plan, just go do it.' This is a view that would not, in general, be shared by some other disciplines. The military and movie-making, for example, are disciplines where every attempt is made to remove as much uncertainty as possible in order to maximize everyone's chances of success. Maybe it's because in the military, lives are often at stake, while in film-making, huge amounts of money are involved. Anyway, for us exponents of common sense, I would argue that removing the dead hand of chance as far as possible is a good thing to do. It means that we bring the maximum sense of reality into whatever venture we are beginning. It means that everyone's expectations are set correctly. It means we have the biggest chance of doing what we have promised to do.

One of the best ways to remove the hand of chance is to lay out our venture on a strip board. In doing this, notice that we combine use of three of the four principles we have described so far – 2, know what you're trying to do, 3, there is always a sequence of events, and 4, things don't get done if people don't do them.

To illustrate laying out a venture on a strip board, let me use the following example. It tries to be big enough not to be a Walt Disney production, but not so big as to be a Cecil B. De Mille one. Let's assume that we are a company with a new product that has emerged from our research department. The research people think it's hot and it's agreed that one of the ways we can test this hypothesis is to find some people who want to buy it. (Notice here the use again of our first principle of common sense – 1, many things are simple. It may be that the marketing department is going to do all kinds of fancy market research on this product, and while in no way meaning to knock that, there's nothing like finding people prepared to part with some hard cash as a way of testing the market.)

Anyway, back to our product. We agree first the scope of this little trial (2, know what you're trying to do). We use the 'understand what you're trying to do' and 'know if what you're trying to do is what everyone wants' tools that we described in Chapter 2 to establish the goals of the venture that will keep all the stakeholders happy. We agree that we will run the show for three months. At the end of that time, if the following have been achieved, the project will be classed as a success:

- get some revenue (we agree that we will try at least to cover our costs during this little exercise);
- get some customers, i.e. reference sites;
- develop some basic marketing materials, sales materials and a sales approach;
- make some recommendations about what changes, if any, are needed to make the product more saleable.

We also make clear that the following are *not* part of the scope of our little project:

- complete, final marketing and sales collateral;
- making changes to the product to make it more saleable (we will make *recommendations*, but not the changes themselves. In other words, we go with whatever research has given us).

Now, using principle 3, there is always a sequence of events, and principle 4, things don't get done if people don't do them, we lay out all the jobs we can think of on to a strip board, as shown in Figure 4.7.

Now we see precisely who's doing what and when. We can test key assumptions – we've assumed, for example, that we are going to target 100 customers and that we will achieve a conversion rate of calls to meetings of, say, 20 per cent. This will mean we have to attend 20 meetings over the duration of the project at, say, two a day, so we can see from the strip board whether enough time has been set aside for meetings. If we achieve a conversion rate of meetings to sales of, say, one in two, then we can estimate the revenue that will flow from our efforts and see whether it satisfies the goals we identified earlier. Also, using the strip board, everyone can see very clearly the big picture and their part in it. It will be easy for us to check progress. On any given day, we can draw a horizontal line and anything above that line should be done. If some things are not, then we are behind schedule; if some things from below the line are done, we are ahead of schedule.

Figure 4.7 Jobs laid out on a strip board

Day #	Date	Strider	Gilgalad	Frodo	Gandalf
1	14-Nov-00	Scoping plan	Scoping plan; writing first draft project plan	3 hrs follow-up on mailer	Establish Web
2	15-Nov-00		Establish web requirements; enter them in project plan – circulate for review	3 hrs follow-up on mailer	
3	16-Nov-00		Talk to AB on Accounts	3 hrs follow-up on mailer	
4	17-Nov-00		N/A	3 hrs follow-up on mailer	
5	18-Nov-00				
6	19-Nov-00				
7	20-Nov-00		Talk to ABC on De, FG on Accounts, HI on Accounts, JK on Accounts; Sales Meeting	3 hrs follow-up on mailer	
8	21-Nov-00		N/A	3 hrs follow-up on mailer	
9	22-Nov-00		N/A	3 hrs follow-up on mailer	
10	23-Nov-00	Meeting those	Meeting those guys – ABC on defining web requirements; meeting DE	3 hrs follow-up on mailer	
11	24-Nov-00		Requirements of project + Tuesday's delivery in that place; Meet DE on marketing requirements	3 hrs follow-up on mailer	
12	25-Nov-00		Sales meeting (present the plan), practise ABC presentation; on phone – get at least 1 meeting		
13	26-Nov-00		On the phone	3 hrs follow-up on mailer	
14	27-Nov-00		On the phone; test presentation to ABC; get feedback from DE on marketing requirements	3 hrs follow-up on mailer	
15	28-Nov-00	Written reference	N/A		
16	29-Nov-00		N/A		
17	30-Nov-00	Meeting other	Sales meeting; on the phone; get feedback on the guys; 12:00 with AB on her accounts; write first draft	3 hrs follow-up on mailer	
18	1-Dec-00		On the phone/Get at least one meeting – arranged for ABC offer to be confirmed	3 hrs follow-up on mailer	
19	2-Dec-00		Meeting AB in CD and EF in GH		
20	3-Dec-00		N/A		
21	4-Dec-00	Meeting	N/A		
22	5-Dec-00	Meeting			
23	6-Dec-00				
24	7-Dec-00				
25	8-Dec-00				
26	9-Dec-00				
27	10-Dec-00				

Cast [jobs]

Figure 4.7 continued

Day #	Date	Cast [jobs]			
		Strider	Gilgalad	Frodo	Gandalf
28	11-Dec-00	Meeting A+B	Get feedback; send letter		
29	12-Dec-00		Get feedback; ring AB		
30	13-Dec-00		Follow up on e-mails for meetings		
31	14-Dec-00		N/A		
32	15-Dec-00		N/A		
33	16-Dec-00				
34	17-Dec-00				
35	18-Dec-00		Sales meeting; on the phone (follow-up); write Knowledge Base 2		
36	19-Dec-00		Firm up on requirements document		
37	20-Dec-00		Confirm consultancy day with ABC		
38	21-Dec-00		N/A		
39	22-Dec-00		N/A		
40	23-Dec-00				
41	24-Dec-00				
42	25-Dec-00				
43	26-Dec-00				
44	27-Dec-00				
45	28-Dec-00		N/A		
46	29-Dec-00		N/A		
47	30-Dec-00				
48	31-Dec-00				
49	1-Jan-01				
50	2-Jan-01		Sales meeting (get a date for training); accumulate customers' response for recommendations report		
51	3-Jan-01		Phone		
52	4-Jan-01		N/A		
53	5-Jan-01		N/A		
54	6-Jan-01				
55	7-Jan-01				
56	8-Jan-01	Agree exact	Agree exact 4 days of NK – effort for next three weeks to include shortening on Web		Agree exact
57	9-Jan-01	Meeting	Meeting		

#	Date		
58	10-Jan-01	Meeting	Meeting
56	11-Jan-01		N/A
57	12-Jan-01		N/A
58	13-Jan-01		
59	14-Jan-01		
60	15-Jan-01		Prepare sales training
61	16-Jan-01		Deliver sales training
62	17-Jan-01	Meeting	Meeting
63	18-Jan-01		N/A
64	19-Jan-01		N/A
65	20-Jan-01		
66	21-Jan-01		
67	22-Jan-01		Sales meeting
68	23-Jan-01		Meeting
69	24-Jan-01		Meeting
70	25-Jan-01		N/A
71	26-Jan-01		N/A
72	27-Jan-01		
73	28-Jan-01		
74	29-Jan-01		Sales meeting
75	30-Jan-01		Meeting
76	31-Jan-01		Meeting
77	1-Feb-01		N/A
78	2-Feb-01		N/a
79	3-Feb-01		
80	4-Feb-01		
81	5-Feb-01		Sales meeting
82	6-Feb-01		Meeting
83	7-Feb-01		Meeting
84	8-Feb-01		N/A
85	9-Feb-01		N/A
86	10-Feb-01		
87	11-Feb-01		
88	12-Feb-01		Hand-off to A/M and DE
89	13-Feb-01		Hand-off to A/M and DE
90	14-Feb-01		Hand-off to A/M and DE

The hand of chance will inevitably still intervene in our project, but now when it does, we won't have that uncertain feeling of 'what does it mean?', 'what will this do to me?'. Using our strip board we'll be able to see precisely what the inevitable surprises on the project will do to us.

In reality, a strip board is like a simulator of your venture. By building or working through a strip board, you can get a real feeling of what it would be like to live through the project. In addition, you can try all manner of 'what if' scenarios before you do them for real.

Example 5 Ensuring that your organization delivers on its commitments

Do you have any of the following problems?

■ You work in the product development or service delivery parts of your organization. From your point of view it seems as if the people who are responsible for promising/committing things to customers always make unreasonable promises.

■ You are a sales person or a person responsible for ensuring that promised customer service levels are achieved. It seems like the product development or service delivery people in your organization never come through on the commitments you have made. This seems to be true even when (a) you feel you have made eminently reasonable promises and (b) you may have even gone to the trouble of checking with the appropriate people – 'Are you absolutely sure I can feel confident in promising this?'

■ You are the head of an organization of the types described above. You have a feeling that you are not getting enough 'bang for the buck', that somehow – although you can't quite see how – your organization is inefficient. Or even – your darkest fear – inept; that it doesn't really know what it's about. You've tried lots of things – training, changes in management structure or personnel, quality improvement drives and programmes – but the basic problem remains.

▨ You are anyone in the organization and you find yourself working harder and harder and every day becoming more and more stressed.

If you answered 'yes' to any of the above questions, your problem may be the following. To put it in a fancy way, it could be that your organization-wide demand exceeds supply. Put more simply, it means that you may be trying to do too much with too little. 'What's new?' I hear you say. I can understand why you might say that. Most organizations do. Indeed, there is an argument that says it's a good thing to do; that all organizations should strive such that their reach exceeds their grasp. For example, in a *Fortune* article entitled 'Reinvent your company', the author Gary Hamel says that the first rule for 'designing a culture that inspires innovation' is to 'set unreasonable expectations'. He quotes a GE Capital executive as saying: 'It is expected that we will grow earnings 20 per cent per year or more. When you have objectives that are that outlandish, it forces you to think very differently about your opportunities.'

Now I have no problem with any of this. Ambitious targets? Sure. Thinking innovatively about achieving them? Absolutely. But not at the expense of losing the plot. And certainly not by trying to pretend that our fourth principle of common sense, things don't get done if people don't do them, somehow doesn't apply to you. I'll state it as bluntly as I can: if your organization is trying to do more work than there are people available to do it, you will end up not doing all of the things that need to be done. And depending on the shortfall between demand (work to be done) and supply (people available to do it), you may end up missing your targets by a little bit or by a mile.

In my experience, the tendency is more towards the latter end of the spectrum. Organizations which have a supply–demand discrepancy usually have a *huge* supply–demand discrepancy. This is particularly true of fast-growth, high-tech organizations

– especially if they have large amounts of somebody else's money paying for their endeavours.

So what should you do? It's simple, really. We've seen the approach already in this chapter. Figure out as an organization how much demand there is (work to be done), figure out how much supply there is (people to do the work), prioritize the list, then make the cut. Forget about all those notions of extended overtime or 'stretch' targets (where 'stretch' generally equals 'impossible' or 'insane'). They quite simply don't work on any kind of sustainable basis. Figure 4.8 lists a hypothetical (product development, in this case) organization's projects together with the estimated amount of work in each project. Let's assume that they are looking at a 12-month period.

Now let's assume that the same organization has a total of 1,892 person-weeks available to it over the same period. This takes into account people already on the payroll, plus those who will be hired during the same period. I think you can see that this organization has a BIG problem. I hope that you can see that if you worked in such an organization, all the scenarios I described at the beginning of this example would be happening.

"Forget about all those notions of extended overtime or 'stretch' targets."

To fix this problem, as the organization must, it must 'make the cut' at the point at which supply matches demand. This will entail the following:

■ continuing (presumably) to include items 10 Support, 11 R & D and 12 Training among those things which have to be done;

■ continuing to add in the project management and contingency overheads;

■ deciding which of the remaining projects it intends to do, so that the total of the projects plus Support, R & D, Training, Project management and Contingency doesn't exceed 1,892 person-weeks.

Figure 4.8   A hypothetical organization's projects and estimated amount of work

Project	Work or Effort
1 Project Abel	8 person-weeks
2 Project Baker	541 person-weeks
3 Project Charlie	48 person-weeks
4 Project Dog	440 person-weeks
5 Project Easy	368 person-weeks
6 Project Foxtrot	135 person-weeks
7 Project Golf	976 person-weeks
8 Project Hotel	1,032 person-weeks
9 Project India	256 person-weeks
10 Support of existing products (estimates based on so many weeks per product)	392 person-weeks
11 R & D (estimate based on so many people for so many weeks)	176 person-weeks
12 Training (estimate based on so much training per person)	96 person-weeks
Sub-total	4,468 person-weeks
Project management effort @ 10%	447 person-weeks
Contingency @15%	670 person-weeks
TOTAL	**5,585 person-weeks**

Will this be a pleasant exercise? No, I don't think so. When they realize all of the things that aren't going to get done, I suspect it will be distinctly unpleasant. Do they have to do it? Yes, I would argue that they do. What will happen to them if they don't do it? Well, you may remember we referred earlier to the hand of chance. If this organization (which is maybe not as hypothetical or as rare as you would have hoped) doesn't consciously and explicitly decide what it wants to do, chance will decide for it. And if you think that's a good way for an organization to conduct its business and go about achieving its goals, there's not a lot I can add.

Just to add one small footnote to this example: you'll notice that we implicitly assumed that we were dealing with one sort of person or skill level. A person-week of any product developer's time was equivalent to that of any other product developer, and we were able to count them all up in one big bucket. In solving organizations' supply–demand problems we first need to solve the problem at this level. Then, when we have done that, we can move to a next level down where we look at how much of particular sets of skills we need. For example, again in a product development organization, we might have to consider how many designers, developers, testers and so on we might need.

Example 6 Coping with interruptions

Have you ever thought how uncomplicated your working life would be if there were no interruptions? You'd plan your week out, establishing exactly what needed to get done, there would be ample time for everything, and you would travel home on Friday evening with a glow of self-satisfaction and a song in your heart.

Sadly, the world isn't like that, and your beautifully crafted plan for the week can end up so battered by surprises, interruptions and firefights that you travel home on Friday wondering how it could possibly *be* Friday already and where the week has gone.

It may surprise you to learn that you already know the cure for this. It's what I think of as the 'hot date' scenario. It goes like this. Imagine that on a particular day you had a hot date. To be as bland and politically correct as possible, let's just describe it as a meeting that you *have* to go to. How would you organize your day in these circumstances? Isn't it true that you would plan your day as accurately as you could, allowing strict time slots to get done each thing that needed to be done? But not only this, you would also do something else. Knowing how easy it is for somebody to spring surprises on you or interrupt you, you would actually allow time for this. Let's say you had to leave the office no later than five to make your hot date. Then you wouldn't plan to be finished by five. No, no, no. That would be much too risky. Instead, you would plan to be finished by four o'clock, then you could either leave at that point, or the extra hour would be there to save your bacon if something came up.

Now, even though we know this, it is not something we do every day. Indeed, we have a tendency to do completely the opposite. Even though we know from bitter experience that every day there are interruptions, we behave as if today – for some bizarre reason – there will be no interruptions at all. Moreover, we are surprised and unhappy when these interruptions then happen, even though all logic tells us that they were bound to happen.

So to deal with interruptions, the common-sense thing to do is to apply the 'hot date' scenario every day. Here's a simple and powerful way to do it.

1 Record, for a given week, the amount of time each day that you put into dealing with interruptions.

2 From this get a daily average.

3 This is the amount of time you should put into every day when you are planning your day.

Here's an illustration. Let's say that for a particular week, you record the following by way of time spent servicing interruptions.

Day	Monday	Tuesday	Wednesday	Thursday	Friday
Time spent (in hours)	2	8	0.5	1.5	3

Thus the daily average is 3 hours $((2 + 8 + 0.5 + 1.5 + 3)/5)$. Therefore, on the basis of this evidence, you are likely to spend three hours per day servicing interruptions. By factoring this into your time planning (you could do it on a dance card, for example), you can ensure that the day's interruptions don't blow away the things you really have to get done. A day like the Tuesday illustrated will still leave your day in tatters, but that's a darn sight better than having every day ending in tatters.

Example 7 Managing in recessionary times

Read this quote.

> Colgate Palmolive has a remarkable record of improving productivity, as reflected in gross margin, virtually every year for the past 15 years, even during the last recession. The process is ingrained, and it pays off impressively: in the brutally competitive, slow-growing business of household products, Colgate's stock has risen an average of 28 per cent annually over the past five years.

The article from which this is taken makes the point that during a slowdown or recession, productivity typically goes through the floor. It goes on to say that you need to stop this from happening and, in fact, to cause the opposite to happen. Not only does this see you through the downturn, but it also puts you in a stronger position when things turn up.

No matter what business you are in, avoiding waste is one of the ways to improve productivity. In Examples 3 and 5, we have seen two powerful ways of avoiding waste. Aligning goals using dance cards ensures that nobody spends time on wild-goose chases or doing things that don't take them in the direction they want to go. Planning using strip boards ensures that we use every day wisely and don't have situations where ventures get held up because somebody wasn't there to do something when they were needed.

AND SO, WHAT SHOULD YOU DO?

1 Keep a list of all the projects/ventures/endeavours/ undertakings for which you are responsible.

2 Make sure that after every meeting or phone call, and for every project/venture/endeavour/undertaking, there is a sequence of events (principle 3, there is always a sequence of events). For each job in the sequence, ensure that there is somebody available to do it when the time comes.

3 Maximize the strengths of the people you are working with. (Not necessarily subordinates. Exactly the same idea will work with bosses, customers, peers or anybody else.)

4 Keep a dance card and use it to get a life if you don't already have one, using the ideas we described in Example 1.

5 Teach dance cards to those who work for you. Then use the dance cards to align their objectives with yours.

6 You can do the same with your peers. This will show you whether what all of you are planning to do tallies in any way with what your management expect of you and what they have committed your organization to doing.

7 Use strip boards as your method of choice for planning projects/ventures/endeavours/undertakings. Use them in preference to Gantt charts and, in particular, to so-called 'project management tools'. (Microsoft Project is the most

pervasive of these.) Strip boards can be built using any spreadsheet package, such as Excel.

8   Do the organization-wide supply–demand calculations for your organization. Then make the cut.

9   Build time for interruptions into your day.

10   Execute your projects as described in the next section.

A little planning is better than a lot of firefighting

The section at the end of Chapter 3 described how to plan any project in a common-sense way using the least amount of effort. This section describes how to execute that plan in a common-sense way using the least amount of effort. As before, there are five steps (see page 45). There is a section for each step. Within each section, we present the step first – what it is, the ideas behind it – and then we tell you how to carry out that step.

6 Use an appropriate leadership style

6.1 The idea

A lot of your project management work is about getting people to do jobs for you. This is where your leadership style comes in.

Everyone has a natural leadership style, ranging from – at one end of the spectrum – hands-on, micro-management to – at the other end – hands-off, leave-people-alone-to-get-on-with-it. Is one style better than another? Should you use one of the extremes or something in the middle? Should you be hands-off when things are going well and hands-on when they're not?

The next section suggests what should be done in different situations. Obviously with people, each situation is unique, but section 6.2 offers some reference points from which you can make your own judgements.

6.2 What to do

1 **Superstar.** The person likes to do that particular job, has all the necessary skills and will almost certainly deliver. Leave them to get on with it with minimal sticking your nose in.

2 **Solid citizen.** The person is happy enough to do the job and knows how to do it. Maybe they don't get particularly fired up about doing it, but there's a pretty good chance they'll deliver. Don't get too much in their way, but neither assume it's all just going to happen.

3 **Dodgy.** For whatever reason – lack of motivation, lack of expertise, lack of time – there's a good chance this job isn't going to get done. Establish as quickly as you can whether it's going to happen or not. If it is, it becomes a 2 – solid citizen; if not, it becomes a 5 – goner.

4 **Trainee.** They're new to whatever it is. They're going to need hand-holding, nurturing, mentoring, coaching, formal training, micro-management before we can be confident they'll deliver.

5 **Goner.** It isn't going to happen. You need to find some other way of getting this job done. *And* you need to deal with the person. Your choices are anything on the spectrum from firing to rehabilitation.

7 Know what's going on

7.1 The idea

The plan that we went to such trouble to develop has served two purposes already. First, it enabled us to understand the project in all its various aspects. Second, it enabled us to make commitments that were achievable and stopped us from undertaking impossible missions. Here we see the third use of the plan as we use it as instrumentation to drive the project.

7.2 What to do

Do this every day:

1 Go down the plan from top to bottom and identify any job that requires some action by you today. These jobs are your to-do list.

2 Do these things.

3 Record in your plan actuals versus estimated, e.g. you said something would take three days but it actually took five days.

4 Record in your plan incidents, i.e. things that occurred on the project that the plan hadn't anticipated. Some incidents will be change control events (see section 1.1). These will require you to create a new plan and to communicate that to the stakeholders. If they agree to this, then this plan becomes the plan that you now work from. If not, then the original plan stands.

5 The other incidents will be handled either by using your contingency (the best course of action) or by working more (not a good idea).

6 From this updated version of the plan you can see the status of the project, i.e. has the end date changed, has the budget changed?

8 Tell people what's going on

8.1 The idea

Step 5(b) set the expectations of the stakeholders initially. Step 8 ensures that you continue to manage their expectations over the life of the project.

8.2 What to do

You know the status of the project from the preceding step. Once a week, communicate this to the stakeholders in a status report.

9 Repeat steps 1 to 8 until the project is over

9.1 The idea

We don't just have a giant orgy of planning and then take a giant jump to the end of the project. In reality we plan and then we move forward and then we re-plan. That's what the routine in section 7.2 describes. In doing so, notice that we end up going back through steps 1 to 8.

9.2 What to do

Nothing – you're already doing it!

10 Do a post-mortem or review on the project

10.1 The idea

Whether the project is an outstanding success, a monumental failure or anything in between, you want to learn something from it. This step is where you do that.

10.2 What to do

1 Be sure to gather input from as many stakeholders as you possibly can.

2 Write down what you did well so you can do it again.

3 Write down what was done badly so you don't do it again.

4 Compare what you estimated in your plan with what actually happened. Use this information the next time you have to build a plan (see step 2).

05

Things rarely turn out as expected

Despite our best efforts, there will always be surprises. This chapter talks about minimizing the number and effect of surprises

The idea

'Life is full of surprises.' There perhaps isn't a week goes by that we don't find ourselves either saying this or being reminded of how true it is. In a sense, a lot of the things we've talked about so far – principle 2, know what you're trying to do; 3, there is always a sequence of events; 4, things don't get done if people don't do them – have been about trying to reduce the likelihood of these surprises happening. Some of the main tools we have described, especially dance cards and strip boards, are about looking into the future and searching for surprises.

Despite our best efforts, however, there will always be surprises out there waiting for us. 'If you don't actively attack the risks [on your project],' software authority Tom Gilb has written, 'the risks will actively attack you.' Sometimes I think we are like people walking through minefields. The tools we have described give us partial maps of the minefield, but we know that these maps are incomplete and that unknown mines still lie there waiting for us.

"This tool is the equivalent of wearing body armour as we pass through the minefield."

To deal with these mines, we need some tools, and we will describe two. The first is the use of contingency or padding or margin for error. This tool is the equivalent of wearing body armour as we pass through the minefield. We know the mines are there, we assume that it is going to be impossible to avoid stepping on some of them, so some of them will definitely explode. What we want to ensure, then, is that the explosions don't kill us. This is not a stupid approach. Not dying is a laudable and worthwhile aim! Contingency is a reactive thing. When a surprise occurs, the contingency (we hope) enables us to deal with it.

However, we can also do a smarter thing. We can look out over the minefield and identify suspicious looking bumps in the ground or signs of digging and say that there is a fair likelihood that there is a mine in a certain place. Then, as we progress through the minefield, we can try to manage our progress as best we can to get past those particular mines. These mines may still go off – and then the contingency is there to save our bacon. Not only that, but we may also have taken specific additional measures to deal with specific mines. And if the mines don't go off, then so much the better – our efforts will be repaid many times over in terms of the number of 'firefights' we don't have to fight. This latter approach is called risk management.

These two tools – the use of contingency and risk management – are described in the next section.

Tools

Contingency

It's possible to make this whole discussion reasonably complicated. Bearing in mind principle 1, many things are simple, let's see if we can avoid doing that. Therefore, rather than trying to get into an exhaustive discussion of contingency, let's converge quickly on a few simple ideas.

The first is, as we have said already, it's mandatory. It's not that you'll only have it on your more cushy undertakings and jettison it on those that are down to the wire, you must have it on every venture.

In mature industries, such as construction or manufacturing or even film-making, contingency is a fact of life, the same way that raw materials or labour rates are facts of life. Unfortunately, the same cannot be said for a lot of the high-tech or knowledge industries that are floating around at the moment. Here contingency tends to be viewed with the same kind of suspicion and loathing normally afforded to a dog turd on somebody's shoe. Suspicion because somehow it's felt that the people asking for the contingency are going to use it to take a paid holiday. Loathing because it's seen as a way for people to take the easy way out, to 'remove the creative tension', to make things comfortable for themselves, to be cowards, to be sissies.

As a result of this bizarre view, the general tendency in such industries is to remove contingency whenever it's sighted. Given that we have already said that you have got to have contingency in the plan, you need to be aware of this tendency and counteract it when it arises. There are two ways to do this:

- either put contingency explicitly into the plan and stop anyone from taking it out; or
- hide it in the plan so that they can't find it.

There's actually a third option, which is to put the contingency in explicitly and let them take it out. Then they have the satisfaction of taking it out and you still have it in. And, of course, if you managed to stop them from taking it out, you would have twice as much and you wouldn't hear any arguments from me on that score.

Finally, how do you do it? Well, here are two good ways. (As I said earlier, they're not the only ones, but then this isn't an exhaustive discussion.)

- Promise less and deliver more.

- Pad out the estimates, say, of budgets (i.e. make the budget bigger than you think you'll need) or resources needed (say you'll need more than you actually need or say you want to hold on to them for longer) or time needed (i.e. add extra time on to the project).

Risk management

While there are lots of complicated approaches to risk management, here's a simple one that gets the job done. First it identifies the issues, then it gives us a way of dealing with them over the life of the venture.

To manage risks we need to know a few things about them:

▨ which risks are likely to affect our undertaking;

▨ the likelihood of each of those risks happening;

▨ the impact of each of those risks happening;

▨ a calculation of our exposure to each risk so that we can deal with the major exposures;

▨ action(s) we can take to reduce our exposures;

▨ indicators, which will enable us to see if a particular risk has begun to materialize.

"There are lots of complicated approaches to risk management."

We will use Figure 5.1 to record all of this. Using this figure will enable us to see what the main risks are on our venture (risks with exposure 9 will be the ones we focus on first). Then, on an ongoing basis, we can update Figure 5.1 to give us our 'Top 10 Risks' list. Focusing regularly (say, weekly) on these will ensure that we stay on top of the scary things as our venture unfolds.

Figure 5.1 Risk management form

Risk	Likelihood	Impact	Exposure	Actions	Indicators
	1 = Low 2 = Medium 3 = High	1 = Low 2 = Medium 3 = High	Likelihood multiplied by Impact (a number between 1 and 9)		

Examples

Example 1 Getting your own way with a salary rise

Before we start to use the tools we have described above, there is a simple way that you can have contingency or back-up plans, using a tool we introduced in an earlier chapter. You may remember that in Chapter 3 we talked about sequences of events and about how there always had to be another way. If you think about it, this is a back-up plan, isn't it?

Let's say, for example, there's somebody who works for you and you want to give them a salary rise. Unfortunately, it's not just your decision, you have to convince your boss that this is a good thing to do. Rather than having just one go at it, you might decide that you will have a whole series of possible approaches and you will try each one if the preceding one doesn't work, particularly if you have already intimated to the favoured employee that they are going to get a rise. If that's the case, you really can't afford to fail, so having back-up plans is even more important. Therefore you might approach it like this:

1 Have a conversation with the boss extolling Bozo's virtues and how underpaid he is. Maybe, without you saying anything, the boss will spontaneously propose that he gets a rise. A bit unlikely? OK, worst case, you've managed to get the item on the table and alerted the boss to the fact that this is on your agenda.

2 (On a separate occasion) ask the boss flat out. If he says 'yes', you're home. If not, go to 3.

3 Gather competitive salary info showing that, for the kind of job Bozo does, he is underpaid. If your boss says 'yes', you're home. If not, go to 4.

4 Seek a promotion for Bozo, on the basis that this seems to be the only way he can get his contribution recognized. If your boss says 'yes', you're home. If not, go to 5.

5 Propose to your boss that if he doesn't want to increase Bozo's salary, there might be other ways to reward him, perhaps vouchers or some sort of car allowance or something like that. If your boss says 'yes', you're home. If not, go to 6.

6 Propose to your boss that Bozo gets some kind of bonus or *ex gratia* payment. It's not the same as a salary rise, but it's better than nothing.

I probably don't need to go on here. If you want more ideas, brainstorm (see Chapter 3) with a colleague for half an hour. Try to come up with 40 or 50 ways to solve this problem. (It's not as hard as you think.) Then pick the ways that you want to try and try them.

Example 2 Risk analysis for a company's business plan

Figure 5.2 illustrates a risk analysis of a company's business plan. You will see from some of the risks (e.g. the first one) that the people who did it are being brutally honest. This obviously makes for the best kind of risk analysis!

Figure 5.2   Risk analysis for a company's business plan

Risks	Likelihood	Impact	Likelihood x Impact	Action	Indicators
1 Poor management by company's executives	2	3	6	▓ Performance review ▓ Training ▓ Quality assurance ▓ Strengthen management team	▓ Departure from monthly plans/targets
2 Under-resourcing	3	3	9	▓ Verify targets against market data ▓ Hire more people in January ▓ Sort out existing staff's dance cards ▓ Departure from monthly plans/targets	▓ Departure from monthly plans/targets
3 Staff get sick	2	3	6	▓ Shadowing ▓ Medicals for new employees ▓ Sort out any existing problems	▓ Increase in monthly days lost due to sick leave
4 Lack of expertise	2	3	6	▓ Training and development ▓ Proper and timely appraisals	▓ Things get screwed up
5 Office space blow out	1	1	1	▓ Begin looking for extra facilities	▓ People unable to find desks or conference/meeting facilities ▓ Over-expenditure on external facilities
6 Revenues don't happen – forecast is wrong	2	3	6	▓ Weekly monitoring and change control ▓ Financial and management reports	▓ Departure from monthly plans/targets

Risk				Action	Indicators
7 Competition	1	2	2	▪ Continue competitor watch	▪ New competitors identified
8 Staff leave	1	3	3	▪ Ensure compensation and benefits packages are keeping pace with industry ▪ Watch morale	▪ Staff exits look like exceeding acceptable attrition rate identified
9 Clients walk	1	3	3	▪ Renew CRM programme ▪ Audits on lost customers	▪ Increase in complaints ▪ Departure by established customers
10 Unrealistic goals	2	3	6	▪ Change control	▪ Departure from monthly plans/targets
11 Data security	3	3	9	▪ Discuss on 7 Dec at special meeting	▪ Hacking ▪ Breaches of firewalls ▪ Theft
12 Brand fatigue	2	2	4	▪ Get marketing to address and make a proposal	▪ Await Marketing's report
13 Cashflow	2	3	6	▪ Keep on it	▪ Departure from monthly plans/targets
14 Market changes	1	3	3	▪ Marketing to keep watching	▪ Departure from monthly plans/targets
15 Recession hits	1	3	3	▪ Run a tight ship – look for waste, unnecessary expenditure, etc.	▪ Departure from monthly plans/targets
16 New market distracts management	1	3	3	▪ Stick to plan	▪ Departure from monthly plans/targets

AND SO, WHAT SHOULD YOU DO?

1 Add contingency into all of your plans using the techniques we described in the 'Tools' section.

2 Do risk analyses on all of your plans.

3 Maintain a 'Top 10 Risks' list and review it on a regular (weekly, monthly) basis.

06

Things either are or they aren't

How do you know if you're making progress towards your objective? Because things either are or they aren't; things are either done or not done. This chapter describes how to know when things are one or the other.

The idea

The ideas we've talked about so far – principle 2, know what you're trying to do; 3, there is always a sequence of events; 4, things don't get done if people don't do them – provide a framework for getting things done. Our fifth principle, things rarely turn out as expected, points out that things will almost certainly turn out differently from the way principles 2 through 4 may have led us to believe. Given that this is so, we need a way of finding out how things are actually progressing.

Again, the textbooks have no shortages of ways to help us – per cent complete, earned value, milestones passed, number of tasks complete, per cent of budget expended, the list is endless. But for us exponents of common sense, there is a measure that comes much closer to the core of the problem. That measure is to say that once we have our sequence of events, and once we know who's doing what, then each job on the sequence of events can exist only in one of two states. Either it's done or, failing that, it's not done.

Now you may immediately raise an obvious objection to this and say that you may be somewhere in the middle of something and that this is a more useful measure than to say 'it's not done'. I would certainly agree with this. However, to say that you're 'in the middle of something' is really not all that useful either. So can we do better than just saying 'I'm in the middle of something'?

Once again, the trick is to break things down and, as we saw in Chapter 3, to do it in as much detail as possible. If you're working on a 2-month job, and you tell me that you're 'halfway through', then in almost all cases this means almost nothing. However, if the 2-month job can be thought of as being composed of, say, 10 or 15 smaller jobs, each of 3 or 4 days' duration, then you now actually tell me a lot of useful information.

"The trick is to break things down."

If the first month is over and you tell me you're still working on job 1 out of 15, there's clearly a problem. Equally, if one month is over and you say to me that jobs 1 through 7 are done and you're now working on job 8, this tells an entirely different story. So too would telling me that after one month, only 1 job out of 15 remains to be done.

Since – it is hoped – you will have already built your sequence of events in as much detail as possible, it should be no great hardship to monitor progress in this way. If, of course, you don't put in this kind of detail, the job becomes something of a black box, where you have no clear idea what's going on inside. It's out of this lack of clarity that surprises and firefights are born. With black box jobs, you have no real early warning system.

Another issue here is the whole business of what constitutes 'done'. Here we can use principle 2, know what you're trying to do, to help us. In the same way that it is important to know for large projects or stratagems precisely what it is you're trying to achieve, it is also important to know this for each of the jobs in our sequence of events. Each job should produce some 'deliverable', something that we can look at or hold in our hand, and say 'yes', the existence of this thing means that this job is done.

Tools

How are we doing?

The first of our tools is the one we have hinted at in the opening section. When assessing progress, we will think not in terms of part-way through or 60 per cent done or any of these dodgy notions. Rather we will break a job down into elements (smaller jobs), and we will then record those jobs as being either done or not done. If somebody tries anything else, we will ask them to break the thing down into jobs which they then classify as either done or not done.

At first, people may find this notion a bit alien and you may have to coach them into understanding what you mean, what you want and why what you're asking for might actually make sense. I think you'll also find people motivated to break things down into smaller units of detail because of the following effect. Let's say you have weekly meetings whose purpose is to assess status. Somebody won't want to be coming week after week and reporting something as not done. Instead they will break it down into smaller components so that they can report progress from week to week.

Are things better or worse?

A variant on the notion of things either are or they aren't is the idea of whether things are better or worse. Things either are or they aren't is an instantaneous snapshot of the status of something. However, we may be interested in how the status of something is progressing over time. Let's say, for example, you run a company and it's experiencing cashflow difficulties. You are anxious to know some key indicators:

- Are costs decreasing?
- Are revenues increasing?
- What's happening to profits?
- How far am I in on my lines of credit?

"You are anxious to know some key indicators."

Asking whether things are better or worse, from day to day, from week to week or from month to month will help clarify for you what the trends are. Graphing the answer to the question 'Are things better or worse?' will make all of this abundantly clear.

Examples

Example 1 Monitoring progress

We have looked at the idea of breaking things down and then reporting the smaller jobs identified as being either done or not done. There is an additional aspect of this which is worth noting. Say, for example, you have a weekly status meeting where people must come and say how they're doing. (These comments apply equally well when the status is reported via progress reports rather than a meeting.) If someone is coming week after week and reporting that a particular job they're working on is not done, the pressure (peer or self-imposed) generated by this should cause them to focus more on getting the thing done, so that they can report that it's finished.

Example 2 Reducing stress (principle 1)

You can use this principle and principle 3, there is always a sequence of events, to help you reduce stress. We saw in Chapter 3 the idea of thinking of the sequence of events as a stack from which we took jobs as they needed to be done. One way we can consider each job is to say – using principle 6 – that either it must be done by us or it mustn't. Now, if we must do it, then let's go and do it. If not, somebody else must do it. In that case, there is nothing you can do about it, there's no point in worrying about it, so just wait until they get it done. (The Dalai Lama puts it succinctly like this: 'If a problem is fixable, if a situation is such that you can do something about it, then there is no need to worry. If it's not fixable, then there is no help in worrying. There is no benefit in worrying whatsoever.')

A variation on this which makes it even more watertight is to do the following. When you've identified that the next move is theirs, ask yourself one additional question. Is there anything you can do to expedite the next job, even though it is theirs? If there is, this becomes a job in the stack for you. That being the case, you go and do it. If, however, there is genuinely nothing further you can do, then that's you off the hook until they get their bit done.

Example 3 Reducing stress (principle 2)

You can also reduce stress by checking whether things are better or worse than they were previously, thus establishing whether things have bottomed out. Are things going downhill or have they turned around and are starting to improve?

Example 4 Problem solving revisited

The 'are things better or worse?' tool provides us with a useful way of generating potential solutions to problems. We can start out by asking, 'What would be the simplest possible solution to this problem?' Then, if it is our feeling that this solution might not be viable, for whatever reason, we can look for the next most complicated one, say by changing one of the variables involved in the problem. This will generate a new, somewhat more complicated solution. We can continue doing this until we have generated a number of solutions, ranging from the simplest to the most complicated. Then we can reach in and pick the one that is most appropriate to our needs.

AND SO, WHAT SHOULD YOU DO?

Monitor progress on the basis of done or not done. Break things down to a lower level of detail where necessary.

07

Look at things from others' points of view

In Chapter 1, we talked of seeing things simply. One simple way of seeing things is to see them from other people's points of view. Almost everything we undertake involves other people. Seeing things as they see them can be a powerful aid to understanding and getting things done.

Questions

For answers to Questions, please see Answers to questions and scores on page 185.

Q.1 You've joined a new organization and you've discovered that one of the people who works for you appears to be seriously overpaid for what he does. You know that he is pretty settled and happy in the organization. You know also that he's fairly reasonable. You decide to reduce his salary to that of his peers. Your analysis is that while he might be very upset about it initially, he will eventually see your point of view and the whole thing will blow over. Is this what actually happens?

(a) Yes, it's all about how settled and happy he is in the organization. That plus the fact that he's a reasonable person.

(b) He goes ballistic. He quits and you end up with a lawsuit on your hands.

(c) It's stormier than you had expected. You have to give a bit and not implement as big a reduction as you had been planning. Then it passes.

(d) You sleep on it, wake up the next day and decide this was a crazy idea. You've got plenty on your plate without drawing this on yourself. You let sleeping dogs lie.

Q.2 You join an organization where your boss operates a 'need to know' policy. He will tell you the minimum you need to know to get the job done. Your style is very much the opposite. Your approach is to tell everybody the big picture and their part in it. You consider converting your boss to your approach as one of your big crusades, but you're not sure how important it is, given all the other things you have on your plate. How important is it?

(a) High priority.

(b) Medium priority.

(c) Low priority.

(d) Irrelevant, i.e. no priority. In the sense that it's just the way things are and you'll have to work within these parameters.

Q.3 Of the following, which is the worst crime?

  (a) Telling bad news to the higher-ups.

  (b) Telling good news to the higher-ups.

  (c) Telling no news to the higher-ups.

  (d) Giving the higher-ups (bad) surprises.

The idea

This final principle is a very old one. Interestingly, it is also common to a number of the world's major religions.

For example, you may know of the Talmud, the 20-volume work that can be thought of as an 'encyclopaedia' of Judaism. The Talmud tells the story of a Gentile who comes to a Rabbi and asks to be taught all of Judaism while standing on one foot. One of the Rabbi's students has the man driven from the Rabbi's door, taking the question to be impertinent or mocking. Unperturbed, the Rabbi replies: 'What is offensive to you do not do to others. That is the core of Judaism. The rest is commentary. Now carry on your studies.'

Buddhism also has a view on this principle. Here is the Dalai Lama on the subject. 'I think that empathy is important not only as a means of enhancing compassion, but I think that generally speaking, when dealing with others on any level, if you're having some difficulties, it's extremely helpful to be able to try to put yourself in the other person's place and see how you would react to the situation.'

Finally, the notion of 'do as you would be done to' is one that is widely known in the Christian faith.

The six principles we have looked at so far are very much about getting things done. More than anything else, the thing that will determine how easy or difficult things are to get done will be how people react to them. If people are positive and well motivated, they will move mountains. On the other hand, if people are not well disposed towards what is being attempted, they will, in an extreme case, bring it to a halt.

The idea, then, is simple. See things from other people's viewpoints and modify your plans and/or behaviour, if necessary, to maximize your chances of success. Precisely how you do this is the subject of the next section.

"If people are positive and well motivated, they will move mountains."

Tools

Put yourself in their shoes

Once again, we can quote the Dalai Lama who describes this technique very simply and elegantly. He says: 'This technique involves the capacity to temporarily suspend insisting on your own viewpoint but rather to look from the other person's perspective, to imagine what would be the situation if you were in his shoes, how you would deal with this. This helps you develop an awareness and respect for another's feelings, which is an important factor in reducing conflicts and problems with other people.'

My editor, Rachael Stock, has put it another way, but no less eloquently: 'Never assume you know everything.' Or to put it another way still: 'Be open to learning from others.' Finally, the point is also made by Stephen Covey in his bestselling *The 7 Habits of Highly Effective People*. One of Covey's seven habits is to 'think win/win'.

Maximize the win conditions of the stakeholders

We saw this concept in Chapter 2, when we looked at the 'know if what you're trying to do is what everyone wants' tool. Just to remind you, the stakeholders are all those people affected by what you're intending to do. Each of those stakeholders will have a set of win conditions. Win conditions are those things that they want to get from the particular venture or undertaking. It is quite likely that the various win conditions will not be compatible with one another. Anyone who has even a nodding acquaintance with the peace talks in Northern Ireland or in the Middle East should have no problem understanding this concept. So, given that the various win conditions are often more or less incompatible, this tool is about trying to find a set of win conditions that everyone can live with. You'll remember we described a way of doing this in Chapter 2, Example 1.

Examples

Example 1 Meetings revisited

Using all of our principles, we can now see how to conduct a decent meeting. We can also use our principles to spot when we've been landed with a turkey – a meeting that will consume everybody's time and be of little value, if any.

To conduct a meeting, you need to do the following.

1 Figure out the objective(s) of the meeting (principle 2, know what you're trying to do).

2 Identify the bunch of things that have to get done to get you to the objective(s) (principle 3, there is always a sequence of events).

3 People are going to have to do those things (principle 4, things don't get done if people don't do them). Thus principles 3 and 4 identify for us who has to come to the meeting.

4 Principles 3 and 4 also enable us to build the agenda, including a time constraint on each item. Using principle 5, things rarely turn out as expected, add in some contingency to give the time constraint on the meeting as a whole.

5 Publish the objective(s), agenda and time constraints, and indicate to each participant what preparation, if any, is required from them (principle 7, look at things from others' points of view).

6 Hold the meeting, driving it to the agenda and time constraints you have identified (principle 4, things don't get done if people don't do them).

7 Prepare an action list arising from the meeting (principle 3, there is always a sequence of events).

8 Stop when the time is up. By then, if you've done your job properly, the objective(s) should have been met.

To spot a turkey, do the following. When you are asked to come to a meeting, ask:

■ What is the objective?

■ Why do you need to go? In other words, what leads them to believe that you can contribute anything useful?

■ What preparation do you have to do?

■ How long will it last?

If you can't get sensible answers to all of these questions, you're probably on to a loser. For your best bet in those circumstances, see Question 1 at the beginning of Chapter 2.

Example 2 Doing the right project

Projects are hot these days. Everyone is suddenly using the language of project management speak. 'Deadline', 'milestone', 'Gantt chart' and so on. People generally start (or should start) projects because of some business benefit that will accrue from them. Being clear about the business benefit enables you to launch the right project. Being unclear results in projects that will invariably chew up time, money, resources and make a number of people unhappy.

We have seen the two principles that will enable us to launch the right project – 2, know what you're trying to do and 7, look at things from others' points of view. Knowing what we're trying to do enables us to identify the type of project we want to undertake. Looking at things from the points of view of the other stakeholders enables us to pick precisely the version of the project that is right for us. Again look at Example 1 in Chapter 2 for more on this.

Example 3 Status reporting

In status reporting there seem to be two schools of thought. Tell 'em nothing is one, while tell 'em everything is the other. Interestingly, the two schools have something in common – both types of report can result in you not getting any information at all on the status of things. In the first case, this is because they didn't actually give you any, while in the second, it's because they overwhelmed you with so much stuff that it's impossible to see the wood for the trees. Principle 7 tells us that we *have* to tell others what we're doing. It doesn't say we must tell everybody 100 per cent of everything, but it does say that we can't tell them nothing.

Now if we're not going to tell everybody 100 per cent of everything, what are we going to do? Well, we must filter what we're saying in some way, but not so much that the message is garbled, misunderstood, hidden or reversed. In my experience, the majority of traditional status reports, whether written or verbal, do all of these things. In general, such status reports give the impression that there are impressive amounts of stuff happening – we did this, we did that, this happened, that happened. (The message is: 'We're earning our money.') Not everything that happens is good stuff, so status reports are always keen to report bad incidents that have occurred. (The message is: 'We're *really* earning our money.') But there's always the almost compulsory happy ending, the feeling that in spite of everything, we're going to be OK. In other words, few status reports are prepared to report bad news.

In general, people are interested in one or more of the following aspects of what you're doing:

- Will I get everything I thought I was going to get and, if not, what can I expect?
- Is it on time and, if not, what can I now expect?
- How's it doing as regards costs – Over? Under? About right?
- Will the thing I get meet my needs?

In reporting the status, you need to tell them about the things they are interested in. And you need to tell them both the instantaneous status – here's how it is today – and what the status is over time – in other words, the trend. Only then can they have a true picture of how things are going. By truthfully reporting the trend, they can understand not just the kind of shape we're in today but also how things might unfold in the future. The result will be no surprises in store for anybody.

Finally, who are we talking about here? Well, all of the stakeholders, as we've defined them earlier. In general, there are at least four that we can always regard as being present. The first is you, the person responsible for getting the thing done; next is your team, the people who are doing the work; third is the customer, for whom the work is being done; and finally, your boss. All of these need to be given an insight – though not necessarily the same one – into how things are proceeding.

First, you need to understand that status yourself. Principle 6, things either are or they aren't, will help you here. Once you know, by considering the status from other people's points of view (principle 7, look at things from others' points of view), you will be able to deliver the status to them. It will be a message that they can understand (because it is expressed in terms that are real to them), that gives the status (because it tells the truth) and that will seek to clarify rather than obscure how things are going.

Figure 7.1 overleaf gives an example of some extracts from a status report. The extracts illustrate both instantaneous status and one possible trend we might be interested in.

Example 4 Marketing revisited

Marketing is all about seeing what you are selling from the potential customer's point of view. Essentially, it's very simple. Your potential customer must have one or more problems that you can solve. Usually, these problems revolve around one of three things – making more money, gaining market edge, or making life easier for themselves. If you can put yourself in their shoes (through surveys, information-gathering by your sales force or whatever), if you can understand the problems they have under each of these headings, and if you can then see how what you sell addresses these problems, you are well on your way to making more money and gaining market edge yourself.

Example 5 Planning and executing a project

If you are asked to plan and execute a project – a project to do pretty much anything – you essentially bring into play almost all of our seven principles. When a project is handed to you it is important to note that you've actually been handed two things. One is the request itself – please undertake the Poisoned Chalice project – and the other is something that I often think of as the 'baggage', or I've also seen referred to as the 'fixed con-straints'. The baggage or fixed constraints relate to the idea that generally people will say, in handing over a project, that it must be done by such and such a date or for this budget or with these resources.

It seems to me that if you try to process the request and the baggage together, you will get yourself into a lot of trouble.

Figure 7.1   Status report

STATUS REPORT

Project: Great Product Version 1.2

Report: 14

Date: 21 October 2007

Project Manager: Frank

Team: Rachel, Debbie, Declan, Steve, Mary

Distribution: As above plus

                      Bernadette, Hugh, Dan, Pedro, Ted

                      File + tell anyone else who's interested

Overall status:

Requirements	Design	Development	Testing	Limited customer release
COMPLETE	COMPLETE	COMPLETE	IN PROGRESS	NOT YET STARTED

Current dates are:

Testing to complete on 17 November 2007

General availability (at end of limited customer release) – 19 January 2008

Trends

Delivery date – change history

Date of change	Reason for change	Into beta date	General availability date
	Original dates	1 May 2007	1 Sep 2007
9 May 2007	See section 1 of the project plan	24 Nov 2007	23 Jan 2008
27 May 2007	Added an extra person for a couple of weeks	12 Nov 2007	12 Jan 2008
2 July 2007	Some improvements due to use of Mary	3 Nov 2007	5 Jan 2008
14 Oct 2007	Slip in development schedule	17 Nov 2007	19 Jan 2008

Because in processing the request, you will be thinking of all the time you're going to need, all the resources, the budget and so on. On the other hand, the baggage will be telling you that you don't have the time, you won't get the budget and that the vast army of people you're going to need is probably going to end up as a man and a dog.

The thing to do then is to deal with the two issues of the request and the baggage separately. First, understand the request, then use what you have learned to make sensible decisions about the baggage. Our principles of common sense enable you to do precisely this.

So let's assume that the request and baggage have arrived. We put the baggage to one side for the present and we focus on the request. Principle 2 says 'know what you're trying to do'. What precisely is this project about? What is it not about? The 'understanding what you're trying to do' tool in Chapter 2 enables you to do this. In addition, if we use principle 7, look at things from others' points of view, we can 'maximize the win conditions of the stakeholders'. That is, we can ensure that the outcome to the project that we are anticipating is the best possible outcome from the points of view of all the people involved.

Next we use principle 3, there is always a sequence of events, to understand what has to be done to achieve the result we have identified. After that, principle 4, things don't get done if people don't do them, forces us to make sure that every job in the sequence of events has a person or people to do it, and that people have sufficient time available to work on this particular thing (dance cards are the tool we use for this). We can also look at maximizing the strengths of the team, as we described in Chapter 4. Principle 5, things rarely turn out as expected, causes us to put contingency or margin for error into our plans.

At this point we have properly analysed the request that we have been given. We have the clearest picture available of how the project could unfold. (Note that we could have represented this picture in a number of ways. It could be represented as a Gantt chart, a who-does-what-when representation; a spreadsheet, a who-spends-what-when-and-who-earns-what-when representation; a strip board, as we described in Chapter 4; or in other ways.) Now we can deal with the baggage.

In general, what the plan says can happen and what the baggage says needs to happen are not the same thing. Then what happens usually is that people throw away the plan and accept the baggage. By this action they are implicitly saying that the plan is wrong. This, despite the fact that the plan represents the best guess anyone has for this project.

Our principles tell us that this is precisely the wrong thing to do. Principle 6, things either are or they aren't, tells us that if the plan isn't the same as the baggage, no amount of wishing will make it so. Neither will ignoring unpleasant facts. The correct thing to do is to say that the plan represents our best shot at this project; now, knowing this, what can we do about the baggage? Can we add more people or money or other resources? Can we reduce the scope of what we intended to do? Is the level of quality we were looking at still required or can we get by with something less? We do this until the plan and the baggage meet. Or to put it another way, until we get to a realistic plan that those who brought the baggage can live with.

Coming back to principle 7, look at things from others' points of view, we reveal the plan to everybody involved in the project, and their part in it. Now we're ready to begin the project and we have defined a game that we have some chance of winning (whereas if we had blithely accepted the baggage, in many cases, the game would already have been lost – all that would have remained would have been for it to be played out).

To run the project, we execute the plan we have developed. Principle 6, things either are or they aren't, tells us how we are proceeding. Principle 2, know what you're trying to do, ensures that we stay awake to the changes in the scope of the project that can occur during its lifetime. (In general, these are things being added for a variety of reasons. For example, they were forgotten initially, or what we thought we wanted wasn't what we really wanted, or the business need has changed, or the market has changed, or there has been some change in technology, or we've found a better way to do something, or we estimated something as being a lot smaller/bigger than it turned out to be, and so on.) Once again, principle 7, look at things from others' points of view, ensures that we report progress in a meaningful way to all the stakeholders.

Finally, when the project ends we will want to spend some time doing a post-mortem, recording what actually happened, so that the process of planning the next project will be easier. We talked about this in Chapter 3.

Example 6 Common-sense time management

There was a theory doing the rounds about ten years ago that said that in a few years' time we'd have all this leisure time that we wouldn't know what to do with. The notion was that with all the various labour-saving devices around (especially computers and computer-driven devices), a lot of our day-to-day drudgery would be taken away from us. The concern then was about 'educating people for leisure'. Funnily enough, you don't hear much about that any more. And try telling it to an urban couple who get up at some ungodly hour, wash, feed, ferry children to a number of different schools or crèches, join the traffic jam for work, work an eight-hour day (if they're lucky) and then do it all in reverse that evening.

Just as an aside, it seems to me that there was a basic flaw in this and a number of other assumptions made about modern society. Principle 1, many things are simple, enables us to spot this flaw without too much difficulty. It is best illustrated by an example. You may remember the notion of the 'paperless office' that was fashionable during the 1980s. The idea was that you would give people computers with plenty of disk storage, high-speed printers, copiers, electronic links and the result would be the disappearance of filing cabinets and paper. Everything would be available online. Now thinking simply about this, the notion is ludicrous. If you give people the ability (using computers, networks, printers and copiers) to generate and pass around large amounts of paper, what will they do? In all probability, they'll generate and pass around large amounts of paper.

We can see the same effect with traffic. If you give people the ability to do a lot more driving by building lots of cars and more roadways, what will they do? Hey, they'll drive more cars and fill more roadways. So, returning to the notion of time management and leisure time, if you give people the ability to communicate more or less instantaneously, what will happen? People will use that ability to try to run their jobs or their businesses faster. They will try to get more done more quickly. So will this have a relaxing effect? Well, you could hardly call getting more done more quickly a recipe for relaxation, could you?

Anyway, back to the main point. Common-sense time management. If there was only one thing that I'd like you to take away from this book, it's the notion that you can't/mustn't/shouldn't allow your time to be stolen from you by other people. There are (I presume) things you are trying to do with your life and with your career. The only way you can ensure that these things get done is if they are given their fair share of time. Unless you do this, these things will never happen and your life/career will end up not being the one you wanted.

The principles we have looked at enable us to build a common-sense time management framework. The framework has two parts to it. First figure out what you're trying to do, then do it.

The latter part we will break down into yearly, monthly (or weekly) and daily things. Let's go through it, using some of the tools we have already encountered.

Figure out what you are trying to do. We've already seen this in Example 3, Chapter 2. If you go through the exercise described in that example, you will end up with a series of things that you want to do. Ideally, these things should cover the full spread of what you want to do with your life, not just the career or business things.

Do it – the annual bit. At the beginning of each new year (or now, if you want to start taking control of your life), lay out the things you want to do on a prioritized dance card, as shown in Figure 4.5. To do this, you will have to estimate the work involved in each of the things you're trying to do. We have described how to do this in Example 1, Chapter 3.

Now, if the dance card shows that there is more work for you to do than there is time available to do it, you must use the ideas we talked about in Examples 1 and 2 in Chapter 4 (Getting a life, Parts 1 and 2) to 'balance' the dance card. That is to say, you must get the work to be done and the time available to do it into realistic proximity of each other. By 'realistic' I really mean two things. The first is that you don't jettison things such as family time in order to make extra work time available; the second is that you don't implicitly or explicitly accept a situation where you are monstrously overloaded. (Remember, a 60 per cent overload situation, which was what we saw in Figure 4.5, means you will have to work an additional 24 hours a week to get everything done.)

Do it – the monthly (or weekly) bit. By doing the estimating above, you will have figured out how much work is involved in each of the things you're trying to do. The other result will be that each of those things will have a sequence of events (or 'stack') associated with it. In addition, if you've done the balancing of the dance card, it means everything you're trying to do is actually doable, i.e. there is adequate time to do it. (If this is not the case, if you are hopelessly overloaded, there is really not much point in continuing with all of this.)

Now, extract from each of the stacks what has to get done this month (or week). Enter it into your diary, organizer, Palm Pilot, Microsoft Outlook or whatever it is you use to manage your time. (You could also enter it into a dance card that was denominated in weeks or days rather than months. Also, while we're on the subject, the proliferation of things such as diaries, organizers, palmtops and PCs means that sometimes people end up keeping their diary in several places. Don't! *Please* don't. Keep it in one place and stick to it!) By 'enter it' I mean show on which day(s) each of the items from the stack will be done. Again, note that the balancing of the annual dance card will ensure that there is adequate time for all of these things.

Do it – the daily bit. It is on a day-by-day basis that you will win or lose the battle to ensure that the right things get done. First thing every morning (or even better, last thing the previous evening), look at the page of your diary that represents today. It will contain a bunch of things that are contenders to be done. Some of these will have come from the stacks that we described. Some will have come from your inbox, but will have been processed via the regime we described in Example 1, Chapter 4. Now mark each of the items with one of the following letters:

- A – urgent and important. *Has* to be done today.
- B – it would be nice to get it done today.
- C – I definitely won't get this done today.
- D – can be delegated.

Now, do all of the As and Ds and leave the rest. Simple as that. But you may have some questions, so let's see if we can anticipate and answer them.

What if you have some time left over at the end of the day? Well, you could start on the Bs. However, a more cunning thing to do is to flip the page of your diary to tomorrow, go through the A/B/C/D business and then begin doing tomorrow's As and Ds. This *really* keeps you focused on the important things.

What if you are interrupted? Go through the A/B/C/D business again. Also, by having some contingency in your day (see Example 6, Chapter 4), you can ensure that interruptions don't blow your day away.

What if the end of the day comes and some of the As aren't done? In that case, they couldn't have been As! Being brutal about what *absolutely* has to be done today is, in a very real sense, the essence of common-sense time management.

Finally, record where your time actually goes. A dance card is a good tool for doing this – just put some extra columns in to take care of it. It will help with your time estimating and planning in the future.

Example 7 More stress management techniques

Keep a sense of proportion (or, there is always someone worse off than you).   This one comes to us courtesy of the 'are things better or worse?' tool in Chapter 6. In general, no matter how bleak your situation may be, it is almost certainly true that there is someone in the world worse off than you. Every day, thousands of people die of hunger, disease, torture, execution, neglect, abuse, loneliness. Most of the things we face don't add up to a hill of beans in the context of these problems. The next time you're feeling stressed, pick up the paper or turn on the television news.

See it a year from now. Principle 7 tells us to look at things from others' points of view. Imagine yourself a year from now. How will the issue that is causing you so much worry seem a year from now? Will you actually be able to remember it? Visualize it and see if this brings anything new.

"The next time you're feeling stressed, pick up the paper or turn on the television news."

The marathon runner. I used to run marathons (not very well, I should add). Now I think you'll agree that the notion of running 26 and a bit miles is ridiculous. It's outrageous. And so, rather than thinking about all the appalling stuff that lies up ahead, marathon runners use – whether they know it or not – principle 3, there is always a sequence of events. Don't worry about the stuff that lies way off in the future. Rather, work your way through the next little job in the sequence. In the case of marathon runners, this means making the next telegraph pole, or tree, or mile marker or feeding station. Then turn your attention to the next stage of the journey.

Talk to somebody. Principle 7 again. Also, as the old saying goes, 'A problem shared is a problem halved.'

Example 8 Assessing things – projects and project plans

Increasingly, one of the things you may be required to do is to assess plans that are being proposed or undertakings that are actually in progress. For example, a subcontractor may be presenting a plan for something that has been outsourced to them. Or you may be asked to make a recommendation on a business plan or the proposed funding of a particular venture. Or the venture may already be in progress and the question is how well or otherwise it is doing. Often these days, these things we are being asked to make a decision on are highly technical or complex, and we may not be personally familiar with the technicalities or complexities. How, then, do we make the right decision? Our principles of common sense can help us chart a way through the mass of data and unearth the nuggets of information we really need.

It seems to me that sometimes people refer to this as 'gut feel' or 'gut instinct'. Gut feel is not a wild stab in the dark but a sense or a feeling that the odds are in your favour. The following is a way of trying to assess those odds.

Imagine you are at a presentation about, or reading a report on, or considering some venture that is occurring on the ground. What do you need to look for?

1 Principle 2, know what you're trying to do, tells us that somewhere in the welter of information there had better be some sort of goal or objective to this thing. This goal must have two main characteristics. First, it must be well defined, i.e. it should be possible to tell, quite unambiguously, when this goal will have been achieved. There should be no confusion or fuzziness about whether or not we will have crossed the finish line. For example, confusion among the stakeholders as to what constituted the end would be a classic breach of this requirement. The other thing is that the goal must be current, i.e. any changes to it that have occurred along the way should have been accumulated and now be part of the final goal.

2 Principle 3, there is always a sequence of events, says that somewhere we should be able to see the series of activities that bring us through the project from where we are now to the goal. This sequence of events could be represented in many forms, and we have seen some of them in this book:

- a Gantt chart – who-does-what-when;
- a strip board – also who-does-what-when;
- a spreadsheet – who-spends/earns-what-when.

3 The level of detail of the sequence of events must be such as to convince us that somebody has analysed, in so far as they can, all the things that need to be done in this project. Pretty, computer-generated, high-level charts don't cut the mustard – unless they can show you the supporting detail.

4 Principle 4, things don't get done if people don't do them, says that there had better be someone leading the venture, and all of the jobs in the sequence of events better have people's names against them. Also, people's availability must be clear. Names aren't enough. We need to know how much of those people's time is available to work on this venture. Notice that with points (2) and (3) it should be possible to do a quick calculation that will test the venture to its core. Point (2) should tell you how much work has to be done, (3) should tell you how much work is available, i.e. how many people for how much of their time. These two numbers should essentially be the same.

5 Principle 5, things rarely turn out as expected. If the venture has no contingency or margin for error in it, send them home with a flea in their ear!

Example 9 Seeing versus noticing

This is an example of a more general problem of how to notice the obvious. Perhaps the best way to go about doing this is to use principle 7, look at things from others' points of view. For instance, try to imagine what your day, especially your working day, would be like if you were of the opposite sex.

Example 10 Mind mapping common sense

Mind mapping is a powerful tool that can aid learning, problem analysis and clearer thinking. As the name suggests, mind mapping produces a record in a way that imitates how the human mind works. Thus, as well as words, pictures, colours and symbols can all form part of a mind map. While there are some simple conventions for drawing them, mind maps usually end up as individual as the person who produced them.

To draw a mind map, do the following:

▦ put the subject under consideration in a central image or picture;

▦ make the main ideas associated with that subject radiate from the central image as branches;

▦ attach subsidiary ideas to higher-level branches.

The figure below shows a simple mind map for common sense.

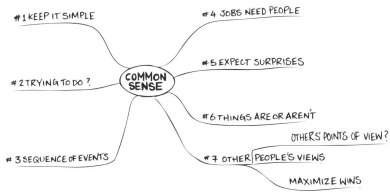

I hope you can see that with mind maps you can quickly generate a large number of ideas on a given subject. In order to keep control of and structure these ideas, mind mapping has the concept of basic ordering ideas (BOIs). Thus, once you've identified the subject you want to consider, the next step is to identify your BOIs. These are the key concepts within which a whole lot of other concepts can be organized. To mind map using common sense, I would suggest two possible ways of going about it. One would be to use the simple questions we saw in Chapter 1 as the BOIs, i.e. who/what/why/where/when/how/which? The other would be to use the principles of common sense themselves. The diagram overleaf does the latter, focusing on the subject of increasing sales.

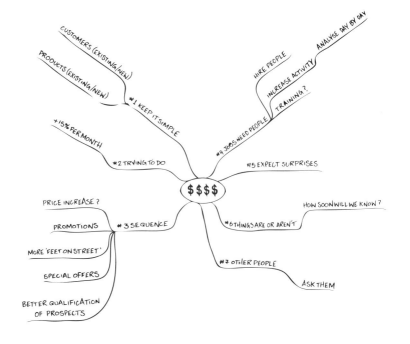

Given the large number of ideas that can be generated very quickly using mind mapping, the use of the BOIs we have described provides an effective way to focus common sense on to any issue.

Example 11 'Gut feel'

'Gut feel' or trusting your instinct is a skill that seems to be held in very high regard by a certain part of the population and treated with an equal level of disdain by the remainder. Studies at Harvard Business School have shown that senior executives of large national and multinational organizations attributed 80 per cent of their success to acting on intuition or gut feel. Other schools of thought seem to regard acting on gut feel as the lazy man's substitute for proper assembly and analysis of the facts.

When we use our instinct or gut feel, the brain considers the vast amount of information it has accumulated over our lifetime, along with all the data related to the current situation. It registers an 'answer' to this problem in the brain. By answer, I mean how likely it is for the proposed course of action to succeed. This is translated into a biological reaction and this reaction is interpreted by people as their 'gut feel'.

By building mind maps as we described in Example 10, we give the brain the widest range of information possible upon which to make a decision.

Example 12 Build a fast-growing company

In the 6 September 1999 edition of *Fortune*, there was an article on America's fastest growing companies. The article identified seven factors that these companies had in common. Perhaps, at this stage, it should come as no surprise to us that behind these seven factors we can clearly see our principles.

These were the factors.

1 The companies always deliver on their commitments (principle 7, look at things from others' points of view). If somebody is a customer of yours, then despite the way it may seem at times, they don't actually expect miracles. (No, really, it's true!) What they do expect, and rightly so, is that you will deliver on whatever they have been led to believe and meet whatever expectations have been set for them.

2 They don't overpromise (principle 7, look at things from others' points of view – again). This is really not too different from the preceding one. In the article, this factor was related specifically to what companies were promising to deliver – and subsequently did deliver – to the financial community/Wall Street.

3 They sweat the small stuff (principle 3, there is always a sequence of events). If you remember, a lot of what we talked about in Chapter 3 was about trying to understand the *detail* of what needed to happen. These days, in a lot of cases, time

is an even more valuable commodity than money. Knowing where our time goes, ensuring that it is spent wisely, removing time wasters, and avoiding having to firefight things which should never have been firefights in the first place, is what this one is all about.

4 They build a fortress. This one is about protecting your business, especially by creating barriers to entry (principle 5, things rarely turn out as expected). Just because things are going well doesn't mean they'll always go well. Maintaining a healthy insecurity about things, always having some contingency in the bag and keeping a watchful eye on the top 10 risks will ensure that your fortress becomes as impregnable as possible to attack.

5 They create a culture (principle 2, know what you're trying to do). This factor is about the corporate cultures that these fast-growth companies have created. In all of the cases cited, the companies set out deliberately to create a certain kind of culture, be it a very formal one, as in the case of Siebel Systems, or an informal one like casual-clothes maker, American Eagle.

6 They learn from their mistakes (principle 3, there is always a sequence of events/record of what actually happens).

7 They shape their story. This again is about ensuring that the investors/financial analysts never feel uncertain about a company, but rather are kept in the loop by the company as to what is going on. Again it's about principle 7, look at things from others' points of view. As the article says: 'When there is uncertainty with this kind of small, growing company, the first thing people do is run … And when one money manager sees someone else bailing out, his first thought is: "What does that guy know that I don't?" They don't wait around to find out what's really going on.'

Example 13 Negotiation

The conventional view of negotiation tends to have a lot to do with arguing until you get your way. 'You don't get what you deserve,' runs the advertisement in in-flight magazines, 'you get what you negotiate.' Negotiation is something you do to other people. It has the feel of a bruising contact sport about it.

A quick dose of principle 7, look at things from others' points of view, is enough to tell us that this may not be the best way to go about negotiating. There is a great book by Fisher and Ury about negotiating called *Getting to Yes*. Based on work done at Harvard, it describes a four-step approach to negotiation called *principled negotiation* or *negotiation on the merits*. The approach has as its objective to produce 'a wise agreement'. A wise agreement is defined as 'one which meets the legitimate interests of each side to the extent possible, resolves conflicting interests fairly, is durable, and takes community interests into account'. Rather than taking up positions and arguing, the approach says: 'Look, we have this problem – how can we solve it in a way that works for both of us?' In a sense, it's the idea of maximizing the win conditions of the stakeholders that we've already seen. The steps of principled negotiation leap straight out of our common-sense principles. These are as follows.

1 Separate the people from the problem.

2 Focus on interests, not positions.

3 Generate a variety of possibilities before deciding what to do.

4 Insist that the result be based on some objective standard.

Looking through our common-sense lens, we could write them like this.

1 Principles 2, know what you're trying to do, and 7, look at things from others' points of view, enable us to understand precisely the (mutual) problem that we're trying to solve. We may not particularly like the person with whom we are

negotiating, but we can see their viewpoint. And we can see that in order to get a wise agreement, that viewpoint has to be taken into account. Principle 7, look at things from others' points of view, gives us the capability to gather all of the relevant data about the issue being negotiated. We don't just get to understand people's bargaining positions. Instead, we see the much wider picture of their interests – the things that are important to them and which must form part of the final agreement. Having gathered together all of this information, we are now in a position to understand completely the issue we are trying to address (principle 2, know what you're trying to do).

2 When we looked at principle 3, there is always a sequence of events, we talked about how 'there always has to be another way'. Rather than coming up with just one solution and arguing to and fro about that, identify a range of possible solutions to the problem. Make it an exercise in creativity rather than a slogging match full of negativity. Keep asking: 'Are there other ways we can solve this?'

3 Principle 6, things either are or they aren't – either the chosen solution is fair or it isn't. Either it satisfies the interests of all the negotiating parties or it doesn't. By using some objective measure, for example equal treatment, equal pain, expert opinion, market value, precedent, we have a way of deciding whether things are or aren't acceptable to all parties.

Example 14 Presentations

You know how busy you are. Everyone else is that busy too – never enough time and so many things to be done. Now, if people are going to give up some of their incredibly scarce time to come and listen to something you say, then you damn well better make sure it's worth listening to.

I don't know how you've found it, but in my experience, good presentations are something of a rarity. Instead I've seen plenty of presenters and presentations that were any of: smug, patronizing, over-aggressive, incomprehensible, unconvincing, rambling, scared, verbose, ran on too long, bored the audience silly, too casual, dishonest, or unsure of their material. The presenter who is authoritative, interesting, relaxed, maybe humorous or dramatic, who believes in what they say, and who communicates that belief, is still something of an oasis in the desert when you come across them.

While you'll always learn something useful at them, you don't have to have attended umpteen presentation skills courses to be a good presenter. Common sense shows you what you have to do to make a good presentation.

1 Principle 7, look at things from others' points of view, starts us in the right place. People are going to give up their time to come to this presentation. Why is that going to be a useful thing for them to do? Presumably they're going to learn something that is to their advantage. But, you may say, I'm making a sales presentation, I'm trying to sell them, something, not educate them. Uh uh, I don't think so. I make sales presentations all the time. And the best ones are those where I set out to teach my audience something and then, somewhere in the midst of it all, put in the sales messages. How many pure sales presentations have you been to that you remember? OK, so this is the first point: you're going to tell them something that is to their advantage. If at all possible, ask members of the audience some time in advance of the presentation what they are hoping to get from it. This obviously maximizes the chances that you will actually give them that. You can do this right up to the moment you're about to begin; however, the earlier you do it the more time you have to prepare.

2 Principle 2, know what you're trying to do. OK, you've decided you're going to tell them something to their advantage. Now you need to decide precisely what your main

messages are. And since it is also well known that people can't remember too many things, you'd better make sure that you have only a handful of main messages.

3 Principle 3, there is always a sequence of events. Now decide the sequence in which you are going to tell them the messages. Research has shown that the human brain primarily remembers the following:

- items from the beginning of the learning period ('the primacy effect');
- items from the end of the learning period ('the recency effect');
- items which are emphasized as being in some way outstanding or unique.

Of course you didn't need research to tell you this. It's known through the great adage for all presenters:

- tell 'em what you're gonna tell 'em;
- tell 'em;
- tell 'em what you told 'em.

Again, research has shown that people remember those items which are of particular interest to them, hence the value of understanding in advance what it is they want to know. This also tells us that we should try to present each of our points from a point of view that our listeners can relate to (principle 7, look at things from others' points of view).

4 Principle 5, things rarely turn out as expected. So anticipate the questions that might get asked. If you can't, have a dry run – this will throw them up anyway. Questions can often take you down paths you hadn't intended to go, and deliver messages you didn't intend to deliver. A dry run will help you spot these trapdoors and close them. Questions also highlight points where your presentation is weak or prone to misunderstanding or is unclear, and so are invaluable in terms of improving the presentation next time you give it.

That is, of course, if you view questions in this way – as a learning opportunity. Not everyone does!

5 Now do it. Use the adage of 'First things first' to deliver your key messages at the beginning. Work your way through the rest of it. Then remind them of the key messages at the end.

"People remember those items which are of particular interest to them."

Example 15 Common-sense selling

Before I had to do it myself, I am happy to admit that I was terrified of selling. The notion that I would be put in a situation where I would have to sweet-talk somebody into parting with money filled me with bottomless dread. These days I regard it as no big deal. In fact I quite enjoy the sense of achievement that comes with having done it well – on the rare occasion when I do!

The key to selling, I realized, is that people must want to buy. And the key to this is that they must have a problem which will be solved by what you are selling. So how do you go about selling something to somebody? (Notice too that in what follows, our analysis unfolds as a sequence of events, i.e. we are using principle 3.)

1 Principle 2, know what you're trying to do, gets us started. What are we trying to sell? In the jargon, we must have 'product knowledge'. We must know all about what our thing does (its features), how it works, and why what it does is of value to people (its benefits). The benefits are the most important. Why would anybody in their right mind want to buy it? What will it do for them? How will it improve their lives? Too often people sell features and not benefits. We must know how our thing fits with related things, either sold by us or by our competitors. We must know all about how it

is delivered. We must know its pricing. If we ask ourselves (principle 1, many things are simple) a few simple questions (What? Where? When? Why? How?), it will generally enable us to winkle out all we need to know by way of product knowledge.

2 Knowing what we're trying to sell, we must now find some people to sell it to. The people who will buy this particular thing you are selling are the people who (a) have the problem you have identified and (b) have the money to spend on your solution. Thinking about it, there will be certain types of people more likely to buy than others. Indeed, there will be an ideal customer, who has exactly the problems you are trying to solve and the money to pay for your solution. Once you have identified these customer characteristics, you can start looking among the general population for these people. Advertising, direct mail, cold calling, referrals, your contacts will all enable you to find these people. The customer characteristics will enable you to gauge how likely or not a person is to buy (i.e. how 'hot' or otherwise the 'lead' is). A potential customer who has almost all of the characteristics is, obviously, more likely to buy than one who has only one or two.

3 Now that you've identified a likely 'target', you need to sell to them. One way or another you need to get in front of them. In some cases – say, if you open a shop – they will come to you. (At least you hope they will!) Otherwise you will have to find a way of going to them. You may have advertised, direct-mailed, followed direct mail up with a phone call, had a referral or made a cold call, but in all cases the net result of what you have done needs to be some form of meeting with them. At the meeting your aim is to establish that they do indeed have the problem that you can solve. Sometimes they will tell you straight up. Sometimes you will have to prise it out of them. The important thing here is not to jump in with

your solution too soon. Otherwise you may end up solving the wrong problem or not solve the problem at all.

Use principle 7, look at things from others' points of view. Pretend you are in their job, their situation. See the things they are describing. Try to understand why the things they are describing are such a problem. Try to make connections (principle 3, there is always a sequence of events) between the various aspects of the problem they describe. Play things back to them – 'So this means that when this happens, you have this problem' 'But that must mean that sometimes this must occur' – to show that you understand their problem. Try to get a sense of what this problem is costing them in financial terms. This will also often have the effect of clarifying the problem for the customer. Try to think of yourself less as a salesman during this part than as a consultant. If you can teach them something, give away some free hints and tips (without giving away the shop, obviously), so much the better.

4 Now tell your story. Either your solution solves the problem or it doesn't (principle 6, things either are or they aren't). If it doesn't, walk away. If you attempt to bluff, you'll be found out sooner or later. But assuming it does – and if you've done steps (1) through (3) properly, this should be the case – present your solution. Show how the various aspects of your solution attack and solve the various elements of the customer's problem. Show how your solution has solved similar problems for similar customers. Encourage questions, just in case there are other parts of the problem that you have failed to unearth. Encourage objections. These show you where you have missed parts of the problem analysis. Not only are they important for that particular sale, but they also enable you to improve your problem analysis and presentation in the future so that you don't encounter these particular objections again. Used in this way, objections become a vital part of improving

your sales technique and results. Finally, if it's feasible, demonstrate your solution in action.

5 Studies indicate that the single biggest reason that people fail to sell something is that they fail to ask for the order! So, however distasteful you may find this, you've got to do it. If you've successfully unearthed his needs/problems and shown that what you have will satisfy those needs/solve those problems, it only remains for you to ask if you now have a deal. At this stage you may end up doing another lap around some more objections. These could include objections to the price. That is why it's useful to have understood the cost of the problem in the first place. If you fail to get a deal on price, there are two possibilities. Either you are too expensive or you were never going to get the deal in the first place and the price is just being used as the excuse. Because pricing is something of an art, this is always a somewhat tricky question. I think that losing some deals on price is no bad thing: it means you are not pricing too cheaply. On the other hand, you don't want to be losing too many. I've seen a figure of 10 per cent (lost because of price) proposed and that seems reasonable to me.

6 Principle 3, there is always a sequence of events, gets us through the final steps of the sale. What has to happen now? Who will do what to ensure that the necessary paperwork goes back and forth, the required arrangements are made, and the product or service is delivered?

AND SO, WHAT SHOULD YOU DO?

1 When you are undertaking anything, remember that in almost all cases, other people will be affected by what you do. See if you can ensure that you identify who those people are, what their views and needs are, and how much you can take these into account.

2 Principle 2, know what you're trying to do, isn't just something you do at the beginning of the undertaking and then leave to go to hell after that. You have to remain conscious of and sensitive to it over the life of the venture.

3 If at all possible, when planning something, try to involve the people who will do the work.

08

Get things done in the shortest possible time

If you are interested in getting things done in the shortest possible time, shortening projects, making every day count and shortening time to market, then this chapter shows you how to use the principles of common sense to do these things.

The idea

We are getting busier and busier. There seem to be ever more things to be done and less time to do them. Those things that we do set out to do always end up taking longer than we expected, costing more and, invariably, containing nasty surprises that trip us up. We end up working late or at weekends, spending less time on the rest of our lives and becoming more and more stressed in the process. As is often the case, Basil Fawlty summarizes it best.

'What was that?' he soliloquizes, in *Fawlty Towers*.

'That was your life, mate.'

'Oh that was quick. Do I get another one?'

'Sorry, mate.'

If you want to get things done in the shortest possible time, with the least number of surprises, if you want to make the most use of the time you have, then this chapter will give you the wherewithal to do it. It seems to me that it's an important enough issue that it deserves a chapter of its own. Coupled with stuff on 'Getting a life' in Chapter 4, it addresses what I think is one of the most important issues facing us today.

There are two tools that we will use and they are described in the next section.

■ Scope and plan projects in a day.

■ Run your project using a 'shooting schedule' type plan.

Tools

Scoping and planning projects in a day

It is possible to scope and plan projects of significant scale and complexity in a single day. I say this because I've been doing it for ages and it has never not worked for me. It is perhaps *the* most effective single way there is to shorten a project. (Actually, not only is the project scoped and planned, but it is also up and running by the end of the day.)

If you don't scope and plan the project in a day, what's the alternative? It looks something like the flowchart overleaf.

This process can take weeks, months or even years in some cases.

As an alternative to all of this, you can scope and plan the project in a day. If the notion appeals to you then here's how you do it.

1 Identify all of the people who are affected by the project – the stakeholders. Each of these needs to be represented at your one-day session.

2 Find a day when they can all come together. Make it clear that you will be regarding this day as Day 1 of your project.

3 Make them do some preparation beforehand. Send them a memo along the lines of the one shown on page 153.

1 Need/requirement/problem identified

2 Proposal/business case/specification written

3 Document reviewed by stakeholders; reviews fed back to author

4 Document updated; various issues resolved by e-mail/phone/meetings

5 Items 3 and 4 looped around a number of times until finally . . .

6 Agreement reached on what to do

7 Someone charged with building plan

8 Plan written

9 Plan reviewed by some/all of stakeholders; reviews fed back to author

10 Plan updated; various issues/discrepancies resolved by e-mail/phone/meetings

11 Items 9 and 10 looped around a number of times until finally . . .

12 Agreement reached on plan

Briefing note for participants in the scoping and planning session

The purpose of the session is to:

(a) Establish what the project is trying to achieve – 'the goal'.
(b) Create a plan for reaching the goal.

The best way for individual participants to prepare for this is to try to do the following:

(a) Document a goal for the project.
(b) Prepare a plan to achieve this goal.

You should need no more than half a day to do this preparation, and should limit yourself to whatever level of detail can be achieved in that time.

(a) Goal

To do this, ask yourself questions like these. (Give yourself no more than an hour.)

■ How will I know when the project is over?
■ What will things be like? How will the company – or my piece of it – have changed?
■ Who are the various people and/or groups ('the stakeholders') affected by the project?
■ For each of these individuals or groups, what would constitute a successful project?
■ Are these different views compatible? If not, is there a compromise set that we can live with?

(b) Plan

To do this, do the following. (Plan to spend no more than two to three hours in total on the first three points and no more than an hour on the last two.)

■ Make a list of all the jobs that you can think of that need to be done to reach *your piece* of the goal.

- Mark any dependencies between jobs (or dependencies on other projects or groups).
- Try to estimate how much work is involved in each job and, therefore, the project as a whole.
- Try to identify people who will do the work.
- Document any assumptions you make or unresolved issues you have.

4 On the day itself, apart from the stakeholders, you will need two other people: a Facilitator to run the session and a Scribe to record the proceedings. (If you don't have a Scribe, then somebody has to take all of the Facilitator's flip-chart pages at the end of the day and write them up. It works, but it's not as good as having the Scribe doing it there and then.) The Facilitator needs a roll of masking tape, four coloured markers (Red, Green, Blue, Black) and a flip chart with plenty of paper. The Scribe should have access to Word, Excel and (possibly) MS Project on a laptop, and a printer, if hard copies of the plans are required.

5 The key to all of this is for the Facilitator – let's assume it's you – to keep the session running to time and ensure as much as can be done is done in the time available. Use tricks like promising breaks or food, reminding them of how much has to be done and what time remains, updating the agenda with what actually happens and showing this to the participants, and pushing things along politely but firmly.

6 Once all the participants are in the room, set the agenda for the day as follows. (Obviously you can refine this based on local requirements – time/duration of lunch break and other breaks, start/finish times, etc.)

09:00 – 10:30   Part 1. Establish the goal of the project – what would be the best possible outcome to this project?

10:45 – 14:30   Part 2. Build the plan.

14:30 – 15:30   Part 3. Do a risk analysis on the plan – see where it can go wrong and what can be done to minimize the chances of that happening.

15:45 – 16:30   Part 4. Assign next actions from the plan.

16:30 – 17:00   Contingency.

7 Introduce and explain your role. Introduce and explain the role of the Scribe, if you're using one.

8 Part 1. Establish the goal of the project. To do this, use the 'understand what you're trying to do' tool in Chapter 2. (If the participants haven't done this before, it's always good to explain to them what you're about to do before you do it. This applies to the things you do later on as well.) Take them through the six questions, noting down the answers on a flip chart.

- How will we know when this project is over?
- What constitutes its end point?
- What physical things will it produce?
- How will the quality of those things be determined?
- What things are definitely part of this project?
- What things are definitely *not* part of this project?

9 'Play back' the answers to them – 'So when this has happened and this has happened and this has happened, the project will be over, right?' 'So if all this happened, we would class the project as a success, yes?' Add the additional detail that flows from this.

10 When they have run dry, this is your first-cut project scope.

11 Tape the flip-chart pages containing the first-cut scope up on the wall.

12 Now, armed with the flip chart again, ask them to help you make a list of all of the project stakeholders.

13 When you have done this, ask them to tell you what each stakeholder's win conditions are.

14 When this list is complete, ask them whether the project scope, as described around the walls, would make each stakeholder, in turn, happy?

15 If the answer is 'yes', then go on to the next stakeholder. If the answer is 'no', then add to the scope the additional things that get thrown up.

16 When you have finished the list of stakeholders, and you've played it back to them one more time, and nobody has anything more to add, then this is the final project scope.

17 Part 2. Build the plan. To build the plan, ask the participants to tell you first the major phases or lumps of work in the project.

18 Now, within each of these, work out all the detailed jobs – as we described in Chapter 3. (If you are using MS Project, use task outline numbering.)

19 Once you've worked out the jobs, you'll want to add some or all of these to each job:

- Dependencies between jobs (definitely).
- How much work is in each job (if you want to know the budget for the project).
- Who's going to do that job (definitely).
- How much that person is free to work on the job (definitely).
- When the job will start and end (definitely).

20 Part 3. Do a risk analysis on the project. Do it exactly as we described in Chapter 5.

21 Part 4. Assign next actions from the plan. Reading from the newly created plan, assign next actions to session attendees.

22 You're done – project scoped, planned and running in a day!

Running your project using a 'shooting schedule' type plan

Most of the plans that we build or that we come across, in most of our types of industries, tend to represent vague hopes about the future. We (lazily, in many cases) 'do the best we can' and leave it at that. Sometimes, we view the plan as an inconvenience that we have to go through before we can start the fun stuff. At worst the plan is a formality, at best a hazy longing for things to turn out happily.

This is in stark contrast to some other industries, and movie-making is a particularly good example. In movie-making, the project to shoot the movie is planned by building what is known as a 'shooting schedule'. The shooting schedule says precisely what everybody on the movie (the team) will be doing every day of the shoot (the project). The shooting schedule is laid out using a tool known as a strip board.

We have already seen this – in Chapter 3, Example 1 on Estimating and in Chapter 4, where we showed the strip board. These sections of the book tell us how to build our equivalent of a shooting schedule. But there is one other magic ingredient here, if we are to get our projects done as quickly as possible. It's got to do with how we view the plan we have built.

In movie-making, the shooting schedule is not a vague hope about the future. Rather it is, very precisely, *what is going to happen*. It is what those responsible for the project intend to make happen. Once the shooting schedule is done, those responsible will do all they can to adhere to it. Any small slippage will be made up at the time. Not only that, but they'll also be trying to *improve* on it. Why? Because in doing so, they increase the chances that it will actually come in on time.

I hope you can see what we're saying here. First, we break things down so that we can see what everyone is doing every day using the techniques in Chapter 3. We then lay the plan out on a strip board, as described in Chapter 4. Add to this a risk analysis of the plan. But now the real pixie dust is that we say, 'This plan shows how it's going to be.'

This may seem like a trivial point, but, in my experience, it's actually a huge mental leap – and a huge mental block. In our kinds of projects, we don't actually believe that shooting schedule type plans are possible. (They are.) We don't believe that it is possible to get down to this level of detail. (It is.) And we don't believe that we can have anything like the level of confidence I'm describing in the plan. (We can.)

It seems to me that such a mental leap can only be achieved, in the end, through brainwashing – brainwashing ourselves, the team and the other stakeholders. If we say it enough times we convince everybody (including ourselves) that it's true. (Because it *is* true. The things I'm describing are possible. I've done them and they work.) We call this brainwashing, 'make every day count'.

There are two constituencies that need to be addressed and they need to be addressed in somewhat different ways. They are the team and the other stakeholders.

The team

There are two points you want to get across to the team. First you want to explain the big picture and everybody's part in it. Then you want to get them thinking in terms of sweeping for opportunities to shorten the project – to make every day count.

To do the first of these, you do the following.

1 Get the team together. Get them all to bring their diaries or calendars.

2 Issue everybody with a copy of the plan on the strip board.

3 Talk them through the overall picture – what's being delivered,

when it's being delivered, the effort or budget involved, how quality is being assured, who the team is, the key assumptions upon which the plan is based and any outstanding issues that have yet to be resolved.

4 Now, take them through the strip board line by line. Ask them to note in their diaries when tasks which they must do, or contribute to, occur. Get them to allocate the time in their diaries. There is no better way to get commitment from people.

5 Next, address the whole business of where the contingency is in the plan.

6 Take them through the risk analysis.

7 Answer questions as you go, and if some questions throw up issues, then do your best to resolve them while the group is all together. (There may be some issues that are only of interest to a smaller group of people, and then these can be taken offline, provided there is a commitment to come back to you with an answer by a certain time.)

You now want to get them thinking in terms of further shortening the project. The points you want to make are outlined below.

1 Do the work of the day in the day (to quote the Duke of Wellington).

Indoctrinate the team with the mindset that what the plan says must be finished today must be finished today. Indoctrinate them with the idea that once today's work is finished, they should go home – irrespective of what time it is. There should only be one exception to this. It is where, by starting tomorrow's work today, it would have the effect of shortening the project. Note that this won't always be the case. For example, if jobs A and B both need to finish before job C can start, and if A is finished and B isn't, then clearly C can't be started.

2 Be hypersensitive to changes that increase the scope of the project.

The project is never going to finish if the team keeps taking on new things. Therefore train your people to keep an eagle eye out for anything that remotely increases their workload. There will constantly be such things, and some of them you may well have to swallow, but many of them can (and should) be the subject of renegotiation (of delivery dates and budgets) with the stakeholders.

3 If people find themselves waiting for somebody else, raise an alert.

In the example in (1) above, if job A is finished, Charlie might find himself waiting around – say for a day. Indoctrinate people that they need to say this. You and they can then jointly agree what is the best way to spend the day. Note that giving them the day off is a perfectly valid way to choose to spend the day.

4 If people are aware of a potential delay coming up, flag it as soon as it's known.

Obviously! But notice that this implies that you (as project manager) are not the only person looking at the plan and searching for shortening opportunities. Everybody should be doing this and it should be part of the culture that you build in the project. Why not offer a bounty for shortening opportunities that turn out to be real?

5 Keep dance cards up to date.

This way people will know if they've over-allocated themselves. It would be better still to use the dance card to avoid over-allocating themselves in the first place.

6 If people can start a job early, do so.

In the example in (1) above, things might not be as clear-cut as implied. Often job C can be started while job B is still being completed. The resulting overlap might well save some time and bring job C in a little early.

7 If people can finish a job early without compromising quality, do so.

Indoctrinate the team with the idea that they should always be searching for ways to finish the job early. For example, there might be an easier way to do something where we do a basic version of it now, and come back and add the frills later. Or we might be able to let something out of testing while it still has a few (relatively minor) errors in it.

The other stakeholders

In the old way of running projects, this was always one of the most difficult parts of the whole business. It generally involved an unfortunate project manager, with a wholly inadequate team, trying to stand up to repeated assaults on his plan by people who didn't like what it showed. ('What's "old" about that?' I hear you ask. 'That's exactly how all my projects start out.')

My advice to project managers faced with these situations has always been to stand over your estimates and not back down. If you're to win this negotiation you have to fight it in the right arena. If you fight it in the 'power' arena – where the person you're negotiating with has more power, or is more senior than you – then there's a fair chance you will lose it. If you fight it in the 'trying to win business' arena – where you are selling and they are buying, i.e. they have money that you want – then you will probably lose it. If you try to fight it in a 'personality' arena – where you try to win it by force of your personality – then you will probably lose it.

The only way, it seems to me, that you can win this negotiation is to show the stakeholders the facts and not back down. You have three lines of defence.

Ideally, you stop them at the first line of defence. You show them, using the strip board, how everybody is gainfully employed, that all this work has to be done and that it is self-evident (from the strip board) that things can't be done any quicker. As you build up this picture in the minds of the stake-holders, they go through the same thought processes you have gone through. They come to understand the trade-offs you have had to make and the constraints you have had to live with. At the conclusion of your presentation, they still may not like the result, but the chances of them then trying to get you to commit to something that is impossible are severely reduced. To put it another way, a strip board presentation of the plan is almost impossible to argue against (unlike Gantt charts, for example, which people often seem to think have just been 'rigged' to show whatever their author wants them to show, especially if they have been generated by computer). The presentation you do to the powers that be can use much of the same format that you used for the team. You tell them the big picture, take them through the strip board and then say that you'll be looking for further opportunities to shorten the project as described above.

If this doesn't work, and they're still looking for the project to be done by a certain date, or for a certain budget or with a certain set of resources, then you can modify the plan and see if the things they're asking for are possible.

- You can remove features/requirements – so that less work has to be done.

- You can ask if the deadline can be extended. It's always worth a try – particularly so with deadlines on, say, 24 December (what will they actually do with it if they get it on Christmas Eve?) or deadlines that occur in July or August, or across other holiday periods – Thanksgiving, Easter and so on.

- You can ask for more resources and see if that will have an effect. (Though bear in mind Brooks Law – 'Adding people to a late project makes it later.')

■ You can see if the quality levels can be reduced. Of course we don't compromise on quality – but we often can!

It should be possible to get this all sorted using the first two lines of defence above, which are all about reason and facts and logic. They are about civilized behaviour. However, sometimes none of these matter. The stakeholders start to engage in denial or in irrational behaviour. They accuse us of not being team players. They say things like, 'Don't bring me problems, bring me solutions.' They say, 'If you can't do it, I'll find somebody who will.' Then we need to say this, 'My plan says that what you're asking for is impossible. However, I'm prepared to give it a try. I don't in any way guarantee that I can meet the deadline, because I believe it can't be met, but what I will guarantee is that every week I'll tell you how we're doing. If it starts to go your way, then that's great. But if it turns out like my plan is saying, then you'll know that you have a problem.' The important word here is 'you'. They are the ones with the problem – not you. You'll be doing your best. If they've been foolish enough to make commitments further up the chain, or to their stakeholders, then that's not your problem. If the first two lines of defence don't save you, then you have to make your stand here. If you do it as I've described, you'll be victorious. (If you don't believe me, try it and see what happens.)

Once the stakeholders' expectations have been set correctly, as we've just described, you can start the project. Over its life, you continue the brainwashing. You continue to try to make every day count using the ideas outlined on pages 159–60.

And as for reporting – to do a status report using a strip board, draw a horizontal line at today's date. Everything above the line should be done. If it is, the project is on target. If it's not, the project has slipped. If all the stuff above the line is done, along with additional stuff from below the line, then you're ahead of target.

Examples

There is a complete, industrial-strength, worked example of the planning and execution of a project, using the tools above, in my book, *How To Run Successful Projects In Web Time.*

AND SO, WHAT SHOULD YOU DO?

1 Try scoping and planning a project in a single day. Do it for small projects first to get confidence in the approach. You'll never go back to doing it the old way.

2 Use a small project again, to try out the shooting schedule idea. Note that 'small' doesn't necessarily imply unimportant. Indeed, the more crucial the project was, the more it would benefit from this approach.

3 Let me know how you get on!

09

Extreme time management

The principles of common sense can also be applied to time management. In the process you can learn how to get *much* more done.

The idea

Here's a way you could look at the world. During your life there will be a whole bunch of things that you have to do – things like doing your job or mowing the grass or doing the weekly shopping. There will be things you don't want to do but have to do anyway – waiting for planes or queuing in traffic or paying your taxes. There will be things you like to do and would like to do more of – spend time with your loved ones or on your hobby or travelling the world or whatever. And finally, there will be the things you really always wanted to do – become a concert pianist or learn to windsurf or climb Mount Everest ...

If you (or any of us) were to accumulate all of these things, you would probably get a picture like the one below. It shows all of the things that, over the course of your life, will contend to be done.

| Have always wanted to do |
| Like to do and would like to do more of |
| Hate to do but have to do anyway |
| Have to do |

During our lives we will actually do a fraction of these things, as illustrated next (which is not to scale).

Have always wanted to do
Like to do and would like to do more of
Hate to do but have to do anyway
Have to do

The things that we will do

If you go on a conventional time management course or buy a time management book, it will definitely make you more efficient – so that you can get more things done. (It would have to be a pretty execrable course or book that wouldn't give you some help and guidance in this area.) The result would be as shown below. The efficiency that you gain from the time management techniques would increase your ability to do more things.

Have always wanted to do
Like to do and would like to do more of
Hate to do but have to do anyway
Have to do

The things that we will do

But if you compare the heights of the two columns directly above you see how limited conventional time management is. For most people the pile of stuff on the left is many (and I mean, many) times higher than the stuff on the right. So if you are to get lots done – in your life, in a year, in a day or whatever – then you need to *not do* lots of things. To be more precise, you need to learn the skill of not doing whole piles of stuff – mountains and mountains of stuff. That is what this chapter is about.

Here's another way to think about things. Most people feel under a terrible burden of stuff to do – in work, or even in life. Picture yourself slumped at your desk. Your head and chest lie on the desk, your back lies open to the sky. Imagine now that you and your desk are actually inside a great big silo or cylinder which is open at the top. People – including yourself – throw requests for you to do things in at the top and these all fall down on to your back. No wonder you're slumped!

Now imagine a different model. Imagine that the cylinder or silo is replaced by a funnel. The funnel has three filters in it. Just as before, requests get thrown in at the top, but now what happens is that they get filtered. Each request is filtered three times. At each stage of filtering some stuff drops out, i.e. some stuff doesn't have to be done. The result is that by the time the requests have gone through the third filter, the amount of stuff to be done is vastly decreased. And so by the time they fall on to you, they fall on to your shoulders – because now you're sitting upright, because now you're not carrying this huge load. Now you have a manageable bunch of things that you will do.

The rest of this chapter discusses the three filters and tells you how to implement them.

Tools

Filter 1 – Learn and practise the skill of saying 'no' nicely

Many things, quite simply, should not be done. They should be treated like dog pooh on our shoe – a look of contempt and then shaken off. Learning to say 'no' is as valid a business skill as knowing how to use a spreadsheet or chair a meeting or lead a team or build a plan.

Not many people take this view. Right from an early age we are programmed to think in terms of doing things. In school we get exercises and homework and projects and assignments, all of which we have to do. In further education this continues with assignments, projects, theses, dissertations and so on. Then we start work and we get job descriptions, key results areas, objectives – all the time, things we should do.

But there's a whole bunch of stuff you should not do. (This is as true in life as in work.) And the science of doing this, or more simply, the skill of saying 'no' nicely, is a skill you need to cultivate. You need to learn methods for doing it and, more importantly, you need to practise those methods. In the 'Examples' section which follows, I list a whole bunch of ways of saying 'no' nicely. In the 'And so, what should you do?' section at the end of the chapter, I describe some ways of beginning to implement this idea and use this tool.

Just one other thing about the phrase 'saying no'. In many ways it's a very troubling expression. Whenever I use the phrase, for instance, the initial response from listeners always seems to be that I'm being 'inflexible/not a team player/uncooperative' or that I'm advising people to say 'Stick it in your ear, Bozo' to your boss.

It's not that. For us the phrase 'saying no' is a shorthand way of saying that we must negotiate. We must explain (using facts, not feelings or emotions) that certain things are possible and certain things are not possible. Much of the rest of this chapter covers ways of doing exactly this.

Filter 2 – Learn and practise the skill of prioritizing viciously

There's prioritizing and then there's prioritizing viciously. Let's take them in turn.

Sometimes you hear people say, 'I have 5 priority 1 things to do, 19 priority 2 things and 47,000 priority 3 things to do.' *That's not prioritization.* Prioritization is saying, 'If I could do only one thing on this list what would it be?' That becomes your number 1 priority. Then you take the remaining list and ask the question again – 'If I could do only one thing on this list what would it be?' That's your number 2 priority. Keep doing this until the entire list is prioritized.

It can be a hard thing to do. Sometimes you may need bosses or other people with whom you work (or live or have relationships with) to help you decide. But that's prioritization.

Vicious prioritization takes this a stage further. It takes the prioritized list and cuts it where the supply equals demand, i.e. where the amount of work to be done and the amount of time you have available are the same. Thus, if there is, say, 40 days' work on your list of stuff to be done this month and 20 days available in the month, then you only do the top 20 days' worth and let the rest go hang.

Another way to say this is the way Stephen Covey says it – 'Focus on the wildly important'. The 'wildly important' are the things that carry serious consequences. Failure to do these things renders all other things relatively inconsequential.

I give some examples of this approach in the 'Examples' section below. But I hope you can see the power of this, particularly when combined with Filter 1. If you know – and I mean really *know* – your priorities and you can say 'no' to anything that is not a priority, then you will get *enormous* amounts of stuff done because all of the dross will fall away from your life.

Filter 3 – A little planning is better than a lot of firefighting

In the end we have to do *some* things! The first two filters clear away a lot of the rubbish so that what remains is the wildly important. Now what you want to do is get these things done with the least amount of effort. That's where planning comes in. The discipline that we've described at the end of Chapters 3 and 4 is valid for large-scale, set piece projects. However, if you've ever had the experience of somebody coming to you and saying 'This should only take a few hours' and two years later you're still working on it(!), then you'll see that this discipline is valid for any request to undertake any initiative.

So, when somebody does ask you to do something – whether it's large or small, with a cast of thousands or just yourself, in work or outside of work – rather than rushing off and starting to do stuff, build a plan. Then, based on the plan, tell them what's possible and what's not possible. Then execute the plan. At the end of Chapters 3 and 4 are very detailed instructions about how to do exactly that.

In summary, the three filters mean that:

- we don't do some stuff at all;
- we only do the things that align with our priorities;
- we do those things we have to do with the least amount of effort.

Examples

Example 1 Ways of saying 'no' nicely

The following ways of saying 'no' nicely are divided under a number of headings. Let me put my own personal favourite at the top. Make a sign that says, in big letters, 'Your lack of planning is not my emergency'. Hang it on your door or the wall of your cubicle or in some other prominent place. I've seen someone walk towards somebody's office, see this sign and then veer away! It's good because you don't even have to open your mouth to say 'no' nicely.

Here are the rest.

Deflecting things:

1 Question why a thing needs to be done in the first place.

2 Deflect *some* requests, i.e. show your boss you're at saturation point. (See what happens when you do.) A dance card, as described in Chapter 4, would be a good way of doing this.

3 Delegate more and let go when you do. (Train the people you delegate to, if necessary, to enable you to do this.) In the home, can you find people to do the job for you? For instance, if you tend to do all the chores in the house, maybe you can give some to the kids – even very young ones. Teach a 3- or 4-year-old to do the vacuuming or the dishes. It'll give them a life skill, senses of responsibility, importance and achievement, and what's more, they'll love doing it.

4 Stop saying 'yes' to everything you're given – always negotiate. Look to revise or decline deadlines.

5 Challenge people's demands for your time/be miserly with your time/be less tolerant of people wasting your time/charge for your time, i.e. find a way to penalize people for wasting it/don't allow other people to control your time: 'I'm in control of my time.'

   (a) Give them alternatives.

   (b) Take turns regarding venue.

   (c) Have appointments rather than drop-ins.

   (d) Have a proper meeting rather than exchanging a large number of e-mails.

6 Make people aware of consequences, i.e. tell them that 'If I

do this, I'm not going to be able to do that' or 'Yes, I can get that done but then this is going to be delayed.'

7 It may be possible for you to do a FAQ (Frequently Asked Questions) or some other form of documentation that will get rid of your most common interrupts.

8 Get people to read the manual ('RTFM').

9 Try not to take jobs from other people (taking the monkey from their back and putting it on to yours). Try to get monkeys off your back.

10 Don't be so helpful.

11 Don't do something that's not in your job description.

12 Somebody's asked you to do something by a certain date or time. Ask if it would be OK by a later date or time.

13 Inform them of your workload and ask them to prioritize. A dance card would be an excellent way of doing this.

14 Question what exactly they want.

15 Do one thing at a time and don't allow yourself to be interrupted while you're doing it.

Getting time for yourself:

16 Have quiet time or a so-called 'power hour'. Some people call it 'me time'.

17 Implement red time/green time. To do this you divide the day into red time and green time. You might, for example, say that 10:00 – 11:30 and 2:30 – 3:30 are going to be your red time. During red time you can't be disturbed and won't take any kind of interruption. This is an opportunity to isolate yourself and concentrate on what's important. If somebody tries to interrupt you during red time you politely explain that the earliest you'll be able to talk to them is when your next green-time slot begins. For certain jobs you might have to put an arrangement in place to cover when

you're in red time. Also it might be good to explain to those you work with that you're carrying out this system. If nothing else, it might encourage them to do the same.

18 Say, 'I'm really involved in this thing at the moment' – indicating something on your desk – 'Can I come back to you at [beginning of next green-time slot]?' Most people will respect something like this. Say it whether it's actually true or not, i.e. whether you are actually involved in something or not.

19 Speak to your boss/partner/husband/wife/children/house-mates/flatmates if you have a backlog that isn't being cleared or an unmanageable load of stuff to do. Ask them if they can help, or better still, tell them what they could do to help. Get their buy-in/support to actions you're proposing to take.

20 Make yourself 'not available'.

   (a) Switch off mobile/set mobile to 'Silent' or 'Meeting'.

   (b) Make better use of out-of-office message and voice mail/set phone to 'busy'/voicemail.

   (c) Divert your phone.

21 Establish more flexible working arrangements.

   (a) More flexible working hours. (Shift your working hours forwards or backwards in the day.)

   (b) Work from another building/location/desk/place where people aren't expecting to find you.

Dealing with e-mail:

22 Turn off e-mail indicator/stay out of e-mail/no e-mails one day a week/delete all e-mails – if it's urgent they'll send it again/keep a full inbox and just deal with the things that align with your priorities/don't keep checking e-mails – check two to four times a day/write better quality e-mails, e.g. always give an action / work from most recent to oldest e-mail.

23 If it's an e-mail, ignore it or don't reply. (You know if it's important enough: they'll resend it and you can always say that you never got it, the server must have been down!)

24 Ask, 'Why did you send me this?'

Meetings:

25 Reduce the number of meetings and meeting times.

26 Decline meetings.

27 Leave meetings when your bit is finished ('Can I do my bit first?').

28 Always have a proper agenda. An agenda is not just a list of items to be covered: it is a list of items to be covered with times allocated to each. Refuse to go to a meeting that doesn't have an agenda.

29 Start and finish on time.

30 Give people who are late for meetings jobs to do, e.g. write the minutes.

31 Rotate the chairing of meetings.

32 Nobody gets out until the deal is done or the problem sorted.

33 Have a standing meeting.

34 Run more effective meetings, i.e. have rules.

Example 2 Knowing your priorities

I'm the boss of our little training and consulting company but I spend almost no time in the office. (This is literally true – it was definitely less than 20 days last year.) I spend about half my time doing training or consulting, and people sometimes ask me, 'How come you're teaching the courses?' – the subtext being, 'How come you're not back in the office conceptualizing or strategizing or doing whatever it is that bosses do?' The answer to this question is that in teaching courses I am doing the single most important thing that I can do.

I have only two priorities. The first is existing customers; the second is finding new customers. Anything else can go hang – and does!

(And in case you're wondering I spend the other half of my time writing. Thanks for asking!)

Example 3 Agreeing your priorities with your boss

When I first met my wife Clare, she worked in a large multinational bank. Shortly after I met her she told me one day that she was going for her annual appraisal. 'That's good,' I said, 'how are you going to do?'

'I have no idea,' she replied.

She went on to explain that she didn't know – and wouldn't know until the actual meeting – whether she was going to get a 'Meets expectations' or 'Exceeds expectations'. I started laughing because I thought she was joking. Here was an organization that had very sophisticated performance management and appraisal systems. How could she not know?

It gradually dawned on me, of course, that it was not only Clare who did not know – many people don't know. They don't know exactly how they're being measured. Bosses and organizations are great at giving out objectives such as 'Keep the customers happy' or 'Make the world a better place for small animals' – vague, difficult-or-impossible-to-measure-accurately objectives. As a result, people don't know what they're being measured on and as a result of that, everything is important. Or to put it another way, the 'wildly important' things are pretty much indistinguishable from the rest.

Now, if you can replace this situation by one where you know what's wildly important, then you'll be able to prioritize viciously. So you need to go and talk to your boss and agree these things with them. They need to be concrete, precise and measurable so that neither of you would be in any doubt whether or not they had been achieved. (Underlying my two priorities above are numeric targets both for days spent with existing customers and for new business brought in.)

AND SO, WHAT SHOULD YOU DO?

1 You've already seen dance cards in Chapter 4. Do a dance card and see how overloaded you are. Let's say it turns out you've got 20 days more work to do than time available to do it. Now start practising saying 'no' using the techniques in this chapter or some of your own. Begin by trying to say 'no' for half a day. If that sounds like too much, try for an hour or a couple of hours. Saying 'no' is an endurance sport like distance running. When you've cracked half a day, try for a day. Then two days, then a week. Keep building up until you reach whatever your overload level was – 20 days in the example above. If you get to here, then consider yourself graduated – you will never have a problem with saying 'no' again.

2 Go and talk to your boss. Have the conversation that begins, 'At the end of a year/six months or whatever, how would we both know that I've done the best possible job?' Tease it out until you've come up with things that are crystal clear and can be measured. (Behind my 'Existing customers/new customers' priorities mentioned above are very precise measures of each – things like courses delivered or value of new business brought in per month. The same is true of everybody in our little organization.) Don't stop until you've both gotten this crystal clear picture.

3 Always build a plan. *Always* – no exceptions! Then use the plan to agree with the stakeholders what's possible and what's not. Then execute the plan.

Afterword

Remembering common sense – Point 1

I've tried, in the course of the book, to keep reminding you of the seven principles of common sense. Here is perhaps another way to think of them.

- The first and last can be thought of as over-arching principles. Keep things simple and see them from other viewpoints.
- Principle 2 is about knowing what you're trying to achieve.
- Principles 3 through 6 are built around the sequence of events which is how we accomplish what it is we're trying to achieve.

Remembering common sense – Point 2

(a) In general, rather than looking for complicated ways to do things, we're going to do the opposite. Principle 1, many things are simple.

(b) In considering any venture/undertaking/project, we need to understand what it is we're trying to do. Principle 2, know what you're trying to do.

(c) Once we know what we're trying to do, principle 3, there is always a sequence of events involved in doing it.

(d) The sequence of events happens only if people do the jobs in the sequence. Principle 4, things don't get done if people don't do them.

(e) No matter how well thought out the sequence of events is, there are always surprises. Principle 5, things rarely turn out as expected.

(f) As our sequence of events unfolds, jobs in the sequence are either complete or they are not. Principle 6, things either are or they aren't.

(g) As well as keeping things simple, we should always, principle 7, look at things from others' points of view.

Practising common sense – Point 1

It'll all be a bit pointless – me writing it, you reading it, I mean – if you don't do something as a result. Conveniently – because it wasn't deliberate on my part – we have ended up with seven principles of common sense. Thus one way you could begin to remember them and, more importantly, to apply them would be to concentrate on a different one every day of the week.

▨ *Mondays* (principle 1, many things are simple). Focus on trying to keep things simple. Try to plan for an uncomplicated day with not as much rushing around as normal. At meetings, if things look like they're getting too complicated, drag the participants back to a simpler view of things. Ask yourself constantly, 'Is this as simple as it could be?' Perhaps extend the simplicity to other areas of your life – what you wear, what you eat, how you get to work, how much garbage you generate, how much of the world's resources you use. Take a 'simple pleasure' that you enjoy and make space for it in the day. Take something that you normally do that day and try to find a simpler way of doing it. Try something off the 'And so, what should you do?' list on page 8.

▨ *Tuesdays* (principle 2, know what you're trying to do). Have an objective that you're trying to achieve today and achieve it no matter what. Any meetings you go to, calls you make, presentations you give, understand in advance what you're hoping to get from them. Review at the end of the day how you did. Try something off the 'And so, what should you do?' list on page 22.

- *Wednesdays* (principle 3, there is always a sequence of events). Think in terms of sequences of events. Align the things you intend to do today with the bigger goals you have identified for yourself. To put it another way, are the jobs you intend to do today taken from the stacks of your various undertakings? After meetings, calls or conversations, ensure that things aren't left hanging there, but that everybody is clear what is going to happen next. Try something off the 'And so, what should you do?' list on page 44.

- *Thursdays* (principle 4, things don't get done if people don't do them). From a personal point of view, focus on getting the things you intended to get done, done. Review how you fared at the end of the day. How did things actually pan out? Did you achieve what you set out to achieve or did other things intervene? If the latter, what can you learn from today and what can you do to ensure that this doesn't happen to you again? If you have people doing things for you, are they clear what needs to be done? Are you happy that they've thought through their sequences of events and have ample time to do what they've promised? Use dance cards on them if they're having problems, because their problems will eventually become *your* problems. Try something off the 'And so, what should you do?' list on page 93.

- *Fridays* (principle 5, things rarely turn out as expected). Ask yourself whether there are contingencies in place on all of your key projects? Have you done a risk analysis on them? If not, do one. If you have, review the top 10 risks and see if you're doing all you can to mitigate them. Try something off the 'And so, what should you do?' list on page 108.

- *Saturdays* (or, if you only want to be a common-sense person five days a week, then wait until Monday and pick it up from there; principle 6, things either are or they aren't). If you're at home, then this will probably raise (uncomfortable?) questions about the status of that do-it-yourself job that's been outstanding for a long time; the washing or the cooking for next week; the homework assignment for the course you're doing or things to do with the children. If you've chosen the five-day week common sense, then keep the focus on whether or not things are really done and if people are claiming they are, how can they prove it. Try something off the 'And so, what should you do?' list on page 114.

▓ *Sundays* (principle 7, look at things from others' points of view). Not a bad thing to do any day of the week. Spend a little time seeing the world as somebody else sees it – your partner, child, parent, employer, boss, subordinate, team member, peer, work colleague, family member, friend. You may be surprised what you'll learn. Try something off the 'And so, what should you do? list on page 147.

Practising common sense – Point 2

Principle 2, know what you're trying to do, and principle 3, there is always a sequence of events, provide *very* powerful ways of tackling any problem. We saw this at work in Chapter 7 in Example 15, Common-sense selling (see page 143). It goes like this. Establish what it is you're trying to do, using principle 2. Now ask yourself, using principle 3, what the starting point is. What is the first job in the sequence of events? In Example 15, we established that it was to figure out what it was we were trying to sell. Now, again using principle 3, ask yourself what happens next? What's the next job in the sequence of events, the next link in the chain? As you identify each job, some of our principles may offer further insights.

Carry on like this until you have established an unbroken sequence of jobs from where you are now to where you want to be.

And finally, good luck!

Answers to questions and scores

Chapter 2

Answers

A.1

(a) 5 points

This is my favourite.

(b) 5 points

But I fully respect your position if you choose this one.

(c) 0 points

I was going to give you 1 point for this, but thinking about it, you really don't deserve any points for frittering your time away like this.

(d) 1 point

OK, I'll give it to you for this (he said softheartedly).

A.2

(a) 0 points

Lots of people do it, but it isn't the right answer.

(b) 5 points

Yup.

(c) 0 points

Nope. See also the answer to (a).

(d) 0 points

Nope. See also the answer to (a).

A.3

(a) 0 points

No. No. No. Of course it's about satisfying the customer, but not at this price.

(b) 0 points

Or this. This is the same as (a).

(c) 5 points

Yes. It's not your job to be a magician.

(d) 5 points

Yes, but make a bit of a deal out of it. You were able to do this for him, i.e. save his bacon, because you were smart enough to put in contingency in the first place.

Scores

15 points   It's easy to get top marks here.

10–14 points   So that if you didn't, I'd be a bit concerned that you sometimes aren't focused clearly on what needs to be done.

Less than 10   Or maybe you don't even *know* what needs to be done!

Chapter 4

Answers

A.1

(a) 5 points

If the goal was stable (principle 2) and the sequence of events was well thought out (principle 3), then you can depend on it. Stands to reason, doesn't it? If things were meant to be done and they weren't, then of course it's going to go pear shaped.

(b) 2 points

There may be other considerations, but I think you'll find that with a good goal and a good sequence of events, this is almost certainly the prime contributor.

(c) 1 point

You can go and gather more data, but I'd be surprised if it materially changed your initial findings.

(d) 1 point

Again, it's a possibility but in my experience rarely the cause of the problem if the other conditions which I've described are present.

A.2

(a) 5 points

It could well be – especially if his time management isn't the tightest.

(b) 5 points

This is the best you're going to get. With the best time management in the world, he's going to lose upwards of an hour a day.

(c) 5 points

You might argue, validly, that it depends on Bozo.

(d) 0 points

No. Definitely not.

A.3

(a) 1 point

Most likely? It won't help, but I don't think so.

(b) 0 points

Not at all.

(c) 5 points

Yep. *Play* to people's weakness and it'll go down the tubes faster than you can say 'human resources issue'.

(d) 3 points

It's not most likely, but it's a close second to (c).

Scores

15 points   While the scores in the second question increased your chances of getting a 15, I think you still did well here.

10–14 points   Nothing wrong with this. You've got a good sense of the infinite capacity for people to surprise.

Less than 10   These are tricky questions.

Chapter 7

Answers

A.1

(a) 0 points

Reasonable or not, I couldn't see this happening in a month of Sundays.

(b) 5 points

He quits? Almost certainly. A lawsuit? You can depend on it. And he'd win too. The payout would dwarf the saving you would have made by reducing his salary.

(c) 0 points

Most unlikely, I'd say. Reducing somebody's salary strikes at such a fundamental core of their being.

(d) 5 points

I'd like to think this is what you chose.

A.2

(a) 5 points

In my view, absolutely. Not dealing with this essentially commits the organization to an *active* policy of ignoring how people feel about things.

(b) 1 point

Your heart's in the right place, but I'd have preferred you'd chosen (a).

(c) 0 points

No. See answer (a).

(d) 0 points

No. See answer (a).

A.3

(a) 5 points

This is not a crime. (Although I fully accept that in many organizations it is treated as such.) Ultimately people don't expect miracles. (Although again, I realize you may be saying that in your organization, they do.) Ultimately, what people really want is that good, bad or indifferent, they know how they stand. In this context, telling bad news is the right thing to do.

(b) 4 points

Provided it's the truth, this is not a crime. I've docked a point – unfairly, you may cry – to remind you of this painful fact.

(c) 4 points

Provided there's nothing to report, this is not a crime. If there is and you're hiding it or sitting on it, you're being very naughty indeed. Point docked as a reminder, as before.

(d) 5 points

This is a crime.

Scores

15 points   This is a very good score here and shows a strong sensitivity to these types of issues.

14 points   Yep, not bad.

Less than 14   These types of things are too important to get wrong.

Bibliography

This list includes all the references within individual chapters, as well as a few other publications I consulted during the writing of this book.

Boehm, Barry (1981) *Software Engineering Economics*, Englewood Cliffs, NJ: Prentice Hall.

Boehm, Barry W. and Ross, Rony (1989) 'Theory-W software project management: principles and examples', *IEEE Transactions on Software Engineering*, Vol. 15, No. 7, July, 902–16.

Buzan, Tony with Buzan, Barry (1993) *The Mind Map Book*, New York: Plume/Penguin.

Carroll, Lewis (1998) *Alice's Adventures in Wonderland/Through the Looking-Glass*, Oxford: Oxford Paperbacks.

Charan, Ram and Colvin, Geoffrey (2001) 'Managing for the slowdown', *Fortune*, 5 February.

Chopra, Deepak (1996) *The Seven Spiritual Laws of Success*, London: Transworld Publishers.

Cooper, Alan (1999) *The Inmates are Running the Asylum*, Indianapolis, IN: Sams.

Covey, Stephen R. (1989) *The 7 Habits of Highly Effective People*, London: Simon & Schuster.

De Bono, Edward (1971) *Lateral Thinking for Management*, Harmondsworth: Penguin Books.

De Bono, Edward (1999) *Simplicity*, Harmondsworth: Penguin Books.

DeMarco, Tom (1997) *The Deadline*, New York: Dorset House Publishing.

Dickens, Charles (1994) *Oliver Twist*, Harmondsworth: Penguin Books.

Eberts, Jake and Ilott, Terry (1990) *My Indecision is Final*, London: Faber and Faber.

European Commission, *Opinion of the Consumer Committee adopted on 8 December, 1998 on the reform of the Common Agricultural Policy.*

Fisher, Roger and Ury, William (1981) *Getting to Yes*, London: Hutchinson Business.

Gelb, Michael (1998) *How to Think Like Leonardo Da Vinci*, London: Thorsons.

Gilb, Tom (1988) *Principles of Software Engineering Management*, Addison-Wesley.

Gladwell, Malcolm (2000) *The Tipping Point: How Little Things Can Make a Big Difference*, London: Little Brown.

Hamel, Gary (2000) 'Reinvent your company', *Fortune*, 12 June.

Hampton, Henry and Freyer, Steve (1990) *Voices of Freedom*, New York: Bantam.

His Holiness The Dalai Lama (1999) *Ancient Wisdom, Modern World*, London: Little Brown.

His Holiness The Dalai Lama and Cutler, Howard C. (1998) *The Art of Happiness*, New York: Riverhead Books.

Hoff, Benjamin (1994) *The Tao of Pooh and the Te of Piglet*, London: Methuen.

Kellaway, Lucy (2000) *Sense and Nonsense in the Office*, London: Financial Times Prentice Hall.

Lovell, Jim and Kluger, Jeffrey (1994) *Apollo 13*, New York: Pocket Books.

Nalty, Bernard C. and Prichard, Russell A. (1999) *D-Day: 'Operation Overlord' from its Planning to the Liberation of Paris*, Conshohocken, PA: Combined Books.

O'Connell, Fergus (2000) *How to Run Successful Projects in Web Time*, Boston, MA: Artech House.

O'Connell, Fergus (2001) *How to Run Successful Projects: The Silver Bullet*, Addison-Wesley.

Schrage, Michael (2000) 'The broadband promise: every e-mail a Spielberg epic', *Fortune*, Fall, Special Issue.

Schumacher, E. F. (1989) *Small is Beautiful: Economics as if People Mattered,* London: HarperCollins.

Schwartz, Nelson D. (1999) 'Secrets of Fortune's fastest-growing companies', *Fortune,* 6 September.

Shapiro, Eileen (1998) *The Seven Deadly Sins of Business,* Oxford: Capstone.

Smith, Preston G. and Reinersten, Donald G. (1998) *Developing Products in Half the Time,* New York: Wiley.

White, Michael (2001) *Leonardo,* London: Abacus.

Winkler, John (1989) *Winning Sales and Marketing Tactics,* Oxford: Butterworth Heinemann.

Wouk, Herman (1988) *This is My God,* London: Little Brown.